Keeping What's Yours

Brett K. Kates

Enterprise · Dearborn
a division of Dearborn Publishing Group, Inc.

While a great deal of care has been taken to provide accurate and current information, the ideas, suggestions, general principles and conclusions presented in this text are subject to local, state and federal laws and regulations, court cases and any revisions of same. The reader is thus urged to consult legal counsel regarding any points of law—this publication should not be used as a substitute for competent legal advice.

Publisher: Kathleen A. Welton
Acquisitions Editor: Patrick J. Hogan
Interior Design: Professional Resources & Communications

Published by Enterprise • Dearborn
a division of Dearborn Publishing Group, Inc.

Printed in the United States of America

94 95 96 10 9 8 7 6 5 4 3 2 1

Library of Congress Cataloging-in-Publication Data

Kates, Brett K.
    Keeping what's yours / by Brett Kates.
        p.   cm.
    Includes index.
    ISBN 0-7931-0746-6
    1. Executions (Law)—United States. 2. Debtor and creditor—United States. 3. Tax planning—United States. 4. Estate planning—United States. I. Title
KF9025.Z9K38 1994   93-38879
346.7305'2—dc20   CIP
[347.30652]

About the Author

Brett K. Kates is a practicing tax attorney and member of the bar in New Jersey and Pennsylvania. An expert in estate planning and administration, pension design and consulting and Tax Court and IRS representations and negotiations, Kates has helped countless businesses and individuals protect themselves against creditor claims. He regularly speaks before state accounting societies on subjects covered in this book.

Contents

Figure List

How To Use Your Insider's Guide to Complete Asset Protection

It is virtually impossible to pick up a newspaper today without seeing an article about a multi-million dollar lawsuit that has been brought against a professional person. In almost all of these cases, the defendants' personal assets—their savings, securities, personal possessions, even their homes—are put at risk because of unanticipated lawsuits.

Such lawsuits are not limited to Fortune 500 corporations. Targets include the doctor who is sued for an evaluation he or she may have made two years ago, the businessman whose corporation inadvertently caused a pollution problem and the homeowner whose guest slipped, fell and sues for ten million dollars.

Doesn't insurance cover these risks? To some extent it may; in many cases it simply does not. Consider the situation of the homeowner who carries homeowner's insurance that provides one million dollars of coverage for accidental injuries. Does that policy provide enough protection if a guest falls and then sues for ten million dollars? How much insurance is enough in today's litigation-prone society? Keep in mind that today's lawyers increasingly urge their clients to seek greater and greater recoveries. Add to that the media hype given to outlandish awards. Is it any wonder that "injured" parties assume that their claims are invaluable, and that in many cases "sensible" insurance coverage is simply not enough?

Threats to your personal assets are not limited to those from allegedly injured persons. The Internal Revenue Service may suddenly audit your tax returns and challenge deductions you took on the advice of professional advisors. The Service's claims that you have underpaid your taxes may call for you to pay far more than you have available. Or, a good marriage may turn to ashes, and a "friendly" divorce may become completely antagonistic as each spouse seeks the lion's share of the family assets. Or, a catastrophic illness may threaten to wipe out a lifetime of savings.

The need to protect personal assets is not limited to those who are truly wealthy. This need exists for people in all income brackets, except perhaps those at the very lowest end of the earnings ladder. If you have a home, a bank account, investments in small blocks of corporate securities, valuable family heirlooms or a special collection of items that you acquired as a hobbyist, your assets are at risk in today's litigious society.

More than ever before, the bitter facts of life require people who have struggled to create financial security to take extra measures to protect their hard-earned wealth—their homes, their savings, their investments, even their retirement plans.

This book will show you how to protect your assets from outside attack and how to do so within the parameters of the law. Just as legislators and lawyers have come up with myriad ways for you to fall victim to a ruinous financial claim, they have also come up with an almost equal number of ways for you to protect your assets from those claims.

Lawyers term a person *judgment proof* when he or she has no assets that can be reached by creditors or other claimants. This does not have to mean that the person in question is penniless; rather, it can mean that the person's assets are beyond the reach of a plaintiff or the courts, and that for the purposes of a lawsuit, the person must be considered penniless.

Each chapter in this book describes a legal, practical, uncomplicated approach that you can adopt to shield your assets from attack. Not every approach will work for every person. Instead, you will be able to pick and choose among the options so that you can come up with the combination that will work best for you. In order to ensure that you come up with the right blend of tools, we will explain the negative as well as the positive aspects of each approach, so that you can make an intelligent, informed decision.

To decide the right approach for your needs, however, you must first ask yourself several questions. Each of these questions addresses the issue of what your most pressing needs really are. If you are actively engaged in a business or a profession, you may fear attacks from creditors or third persons who claim to have been injured by you in your business or professional capacity. On the other hand, you may be more concerned with income or estate taxes. Or, you may have a reason to be more concerned with the possibility of a catastrophic illness. By identifying your specific needs, you will be able to evaluate more fully the advisability of using the various approaches set out in this book. The questions you should ask yourself are:

- *Are you engaged in a business or a profession?* If so, you will want to consider the approaches in this book that protect your assets from attack by creditors and other individuals. Those other individuals may be people who have suffered a physical or financial injury. The physical injury may arise because of your alleged malpractice (if you are a doctor, dentist or therapist) or because of alleged negligence in the way your business or home is operated or maintained (e.g., the person who falls because of a crack in your sidewalk). A financial injury can arise if you and/or your business fail to pay your bills.

- *Do your most pressing needs involve the income taxes you are forced to pay?* If so, several of the approaches described in this book could be especially useful for you. By the same token, several may work against you. We've taken care to point out which approaches have special income tax significance.

- *Are you particularly concerned with the drain estate taxes may cause when those for whom you've worked to provide a good life inherit your hard-earned assets?* Again, some of the approaches we describe are designed to protect your assets from estate taxes; some do not offer any protection. We've noted which are which as we discuss each approach.

- *Do you have reason to be concerned with the possibility of a catastrophic illness?* If you are realistic and over the age of 50, you should be concerned about a catastrophic illness causing a drain on your assets. As we note in Chapter 7, seven out of every ten people will be forced to come to grips with the need for long-term care in their lifetime. There are special approaches you can adopt to ensure that your assets provide you with income while ensuring that the principal generating that income does not fall prey to the claims of health-care providers.

Finally, there is one caution that we must state clearly, strongly and without reservation. Complete asset protection is not a one-person task. A sound program has tax and liability aspects that require professional expertise. Many of the approaches described in this book are based on state legislation; but not all states have the same laws. You should ask your lawyer to review any program that you seek to adopt. Similarly, transactions involving your assets could have income and estate tax consequences. It would be foolhardy of you to adopt a program that has tax implications without consulting a professional tax advisor.

This book is intended to give you the ability to map out a powerful asset protection stronghold capable of withstanding even the most brutal attack. The actual construction of that stronghold is something that you will want to do in conjunction with your professional advisors.

The Concept of Asset Protection

We live in unsettled times. Many people who once had secure jobs now find themselves out of work. Within a short time the newly unemployed use up their savings just to pay for the bare necessities. Soon they find their other assets subjected to the claims of creditors.

Equally dangerous to those who have struggled to amass a personal fortune is the fact that we now live in a society enthralled with the idea of making a fortune through litigation. The least of alleged wrongs can lead to a lawsuit in which hundreds of thousands, if not millions, of dollars are sought. I've taught a course for financial planners on risk management and insurance. The course was successful because its primary focus was risk recognition.

Asset protection is based on the recognition of risk and the structuring of your holdings in a manner that will reduce your exposure to risk. The key to risk avoidance, however, is to recognize that attacks on your assets can come from virtually any direction. The list of possible sources of attack includes:

1. Automobile accidents
2. Property accidents, e.g., a business or personal guest falls down a flight of steps
3. Tax liabilities
4. Debts of your business
5. Contract difficulties
6. Child support
7. Alimony

8. Forfeiture of financing notes

9. Malpractice

10. Business breakups

11. The cost of paying the estate of a partner

12. Collapse or takeover of your banking institution

This is a partial list, limited only by the imagination of your creditor's attorney. This guide has been designed to help you structure your holdings so that you can minimize the chances of your creditors taking them from you.

To my way of thinking, one of life's tragedies occurs when individuals or families lose their assets. That tragedy is compounded by the fact that we can protect our assets if we are willing to invest some time and thought in *preventive medicine*. The best approach is to put your plan into action before a claim arises. As you will see when we discuss the issue of fraudulent transfer, if you wait until your creditors attack, you may have waited too long to mount an effective counterattack.

Asset Protection Rules and Strategies

1. Plan ahead.

Many strategies only limit the damage once a claim against assets is made. Planning before the claim is made will provide you with more options and a greater chance of surviving an attack by a creditor. If you try to transfer property after a judgment, your efforts will prove fruitless. Before you undertake any venture—particularly a business venture—try to select a business form that insulates you from liability (see Chapter 8).

2. Review your plan regularly.

The law is a living thing and changes constantly. Tax laws are amended almost every year. While it might appear that some laws have not been changed since the 1800s, don't let the dust of old laws lull you into a false sense of security. You will do yourself and your loved ones an injustice if you do not maintain, review and update your program at least once a year. Should some event occur that will dramatically alter your asset picture, you must review your plan immediately. Changes for which you should be on the alert may be positive—inheriting money, winning the lottery—or negative—becoming the target of a lawsuit.

3. Include your whole family.

Just as none of us lives our lives in a vacuum, you should not review your plan in a vacuum. Examine your plan with those family members who have an active interest in your assets and who may have to react to potential problems with speed and decisiveness. Asset protection is not for the individual. It is based on maintaining the maximum asset value within the entire family unit. You will see that it sometimes makes sense to place assets in certain family members' hands. Clear communication will limit any misunderstanding or resentment as to the use of the assets and for whose benefit the assets will be held.

A lack of communication can be disastrous. I had a client who passed away. He was secretive by nature and did not believe in having a will or entrusting any information to his wife. While he did not have an asset protection problem, this lack of communication and lack of trust and confidence in his wife and children created an unnecessarily lengthy delay in resolving his estate. It also resulted in expensive legal fees.

4. Strategize by objective.

Many businesses utilize *management by objectives* to determine their strategies. You must do the same. Some asset protection approaches conflict directly with the business goals or tax or estate plans that you may already have in place. In some instances, a particular asset protection tool may hinder your ability to do business. Decide what is important to you, and develop your strategy with that goal in mind.

As previously noted, preventive planning is vital. Most businesses that have failed were run by passive managements that acted only in response to emergencies. Take a lesson from winning companies, and control your destiny. If you are passive and simply seek to put out fires, you will be badly burned. For asset protection purposes, if there is a fire it is usually too late to take corrective action.

5. Take stock of your property.

No plan can be created in a vacuum. Guessing can be as damaging as having no plan at all. As with any estate plan, you must inventory the following assets:

- Bank accounts
- Pension and retirement plans
- Insurance policies
- Stocks and bonds
- Real estate holdings
- Inheritances
- Antiques, art and other collectibles and collections
- Other personal property (assets other than real estate)
- Loans you may have made to others
- Business holdings
- Partnership interests

By the same token, you must inventory your liabilities, including:

- Mortgages on real estate you own
- Installment loans
- Credit card and revolving charge account debt
- Notes you may have guaranteed or for which you are a cosigner
- Current lawsuits that may have been brought against you
- Alimony and/or child support agreements

6. Be prepared to compromise.

The most effective asset protection program calls for you to own no assets. The least effective protection program permits you to own everything in your name. Somewhere between these two extremes is the strategy most appropriate for you. The greater the amount of control you relinquish, the greater the protection your property acquires. Only you can measure how much control you can comfortably sacrifice. But, if you want to create an effective asset protection program, you must give up some amount of control.

7. Build a team.

Asset protection is a team approach. Not only will your family be involved, but your attorney will be needed to help you structure your ownership correctly. We provide a trust agreement in this book; however, it is still advisable to have an attorney and financial advisors versed in asset protection review your strategy. Although most states do not recognize specialties for lawyers, search for one with experience. A little money invested now can pay tremendous dividends. As one advertisement used to say, "Pay me now, or pay me later." You must make the same decision if you want to protect your family wealth.

8. Be flexible, be smart.

Asset protection uses the law to your advantage, not for your creditor's purposes. No plan is cast in concrete. Do not be afraid to use as many of the asset protection tools as are needed for your purposes, and do not be afraid to alter your program if changes in the law weaken a tool in your arsenal.

But remember, asset protection is your shield. Never use asset protection as an attack weapon. Although it may seem that the impact of a program is aggressive, if you flaunt your protection a court may choose to ignore the formalities and pierce your shield.

Fraudulent Transfers

Often a debtor will seek to shield assets from a creditor's collection efforts by either hiding or shifting the assets to an *unrelated* outside or third party. Generally the shift to an outside party is conditioned on the debtor's being able to reclaim the property at a later time—that is, when the heat is off. Typically, the recipient of the property pays less than the property's fair market value, where fair market value is understood to mean the price at which a willing buyer would buy and a willing seller would sell when neither individual is required to buy or sell. The concept of *fair market value* is vital to the determination of whether a fraudulent transfer has occurred.

There are occasions when debtors transfer property for less than fair market value without any intent of defrauding creditors. Typically this can happen in two situations. First, a gift of property to a relative for less than adequate consideration usually is not made with the intent to defraud creditors or with the preconceived idea that the debtor will reacquire the property at a later date. Second, the debtor's financial situation may be such that he or she is willing to sell property at a bargain basement price in order to raise cash quickly. If such a sale is made to offset outstanding debts and the proceeds of the sale are used for that purpose, a creditor will be hard pressed to demonstrate that the sale was a fraudulent transfer.

Most states have either adopted the Uniform Fraudulent Conveyance Act (UFCA) or the Uniform Fraudulent Transfer Act (UFTA). Since its approval in 1984, the UFTA has been adopted by half the states in the country. The UFTA, by its terms, involves personal property and real estate transfers that the statute defines as fraudulent.

A shift of property or the assumption of a burden or debt with the actual intent to delay, frustrate or defraud present or future creditors is a fraudulent transfer.

The UFTA also condemns *constructive fraud*. There are three situations, in which a transfer may be considered constructively fraudulent:

1. The debtor was insolvent or will be made insolvent by the transfer or the additional obligation.

2. The debtor had the actual intent to assume more debt than he or she could repay.

3. The debtor incurs an additional obligation in return for *unreasonably* small assets.

The judgment creditor initially has the burden of demonstrating that the transfer by the debtor rendered the debtor judgment proof. Thereafter, the burden shifts to the debtor to demonstrate that any shifting of assets was not a fraudulent transfer. If the debtor is unable to overcome the presumption that the transfer was fraudulent, the judgment creditor may proceed to execute against the transferred property regardless of whose hands the property is in, or by court order, force the cancellation of the original transfer. In essence, the recipient of property in a fraudulent conveyance is exposed to what is known as *transferee liability*.

In addition, fraudulent conveyance laws allow creditors to attempt to attach property that is in jeopardy of being fraudulently transferred. This requires a court to exercise its equitable powers to:

- prohibit a transfer,
- appoint a receiver to hold the property during the pending litigation, or
- issue a restraining order.

All of these remedies are extraordinary and usually arise only in emergency situations. Courts are generally reluctant to grant such sweeping protection to a creditor, since it grants a creditor the status of a *judgment creditor* before a trial on the merits of the creditor's claim.

The theory under which the fraudulent conveyance laws grant the courts such sweeping power is that creditors may be irreparably harmed if the property is not conserved or protected to ensure that it remains available to satisfy a judgment.

Under the law, a fraudulent conveyance will be presumed where an "insolvent" debtor gifts property to his or her children. By nature of the fact that the transfer is a "gift," it is clear that the creditor received no consideration. In other words, the debtor transferred for less than fair market value property that is equitably owned by his or her creditors. The law considers the creditors the owners of the debtor's property when the debtor is insolvent—even though the debtor still legally owns the property. In this situation the law does not require the debtor to have a bad intent. The fact that the property was transferred—even with the honest intention of making it a gift—and the transfer was for less than fair market value constitute a fraudulent transfer entitling creditors to obtain "their" property.

Tip

Fair value is determined by the situation. "Retail price" is not necessarily the market price. Fair value at a distress or bankruptcy sale is usually far less than the fair value that could be expected from an arm's-length sale.

Fair market value is an imprecise term. It generally has been interpreted by the courts to mean what a willing buyer would pay and a willing seller accept when neither party is under the obligation to buy or sell. However, the courts have also recognized that this standard does not define a number, but only generates a reasonable range for value. The issue arises when property has a readily determinable value, so that receiving less than the benchmark price raises the specter of a fraudulent conveyance.

A prime example of this situation would be the sale of a bond that is publicly traded. Such a security has an easily determined trading price at any given time. If a debtor sells a bond in a private transaction for less than the market price, it is likely that a fraudulent transfer will be found.

Conversely, some property does not have an easily determined fair market value. Antiques and collectibles are prime examples of such property. The price an item would bring at sale is tied to extrinsic issues, such as demand, quality, quantity and the general economy. Consider the real estate market, and you will readily see that what may have been a distress price only last year may be considered a very good price in today's market.

Under the UFTA, if the debtor can prove that he or she received fair value for the transferred property or the incurred debt—even if there was actual intent to delay, frustrate or defraud present or future creditors—that is a complete defense to a claim of fraudulent transfer. However, this fair value defense may not apply in bankruptcy.

Accordingly, fair value and consideration are extremely fact and situation sensitive. There are no strict guidelines. To the contrary, reasonable differences should be expected to occur. Your individual situation must be guided by a *reasonable man* standard, giving particular attention to recognizing that purchasers may be aware of your financial need. A *motivated* seller can be expected to receive less than a seller not under the obligation to sell.

At the outset of this section we raised the issue of transferee liability. Does that mean that all recipients of property from insolvent debtors are subject to losing what they purchased? No. The Uniform Fraudulent Conveyance Act (UFCA) protects buyers who act in good faith. The good faith buyer takes his or her title clear of any claims of creditors of the original debtor.

What makes someone a good faith purchaser? The UFCA has developed three standards, all of which must be met by the purchaser:

1. The buyer must have bought the property in "good faith", i.e., the transaction must be a true purchase. As previously discussed, the buyer must not have an arrangement to return the property to the debtor when the "heat is off."

2. The buyer must be unaware of the fact that the debtor entered into the transfer in order to defraud creditors. This standard is tied directly to the issue of good faith. If a buyer knows that the sale constitutes a fraud on creditors of the seller, the buyer cannot be a good faith purchaser.

3. Fair value must be paid for the property. Should the buyer be too good a negotiator, he or she may lose the property to the creditors of the seller. Often, the courts will recognize a distress price, but at certain levels the courts will cease to recognize the sale as bona fide.

If you are a good faith purchaser who has cut too good a deal, you will not lose all of your funds. You are entitled to be reimbursed for the full amount of the price you paid, or you will be granted a lien against the property until you are made whole. The benefit of your good negotiations is lost, but not your money.

Unlike UFCA, UFTA provides a statute of limitations on claims challenging the transfer. A creditor cannot sit on its rights too long. Generally, the statute of limitations is not longer than four years, and in some situations the limitation period is only one year. Check your local state statutes for the time limit in your state.

How Criminal Laws Reach the Fraudulent Debtor

Creditors are also resorting to the use of criminal courts for help in collecting their debts. Many states have statutes making it a crime to issue a check if there are insufficient funds to cover the check. I am aware of one professional who almost lost his license to sell insurance when his check "bounced." The creditor filed a *theft by deception* charge that was only dropped on the eve of the professional's indictment, when he paid the bill.

One client of mine had loaned his employer money to keep the business afloat. The loan was for almost all of my client's savings and was supposed to be secured by certificates of title to boats. When the loan was not repaid and we proceeded to instigate a lawsuit, the debtor filed for bankruptcy, thereby stopping our action (see Chapter 5). At the bankruptcy hearing, however, the debtor admitted that the business had sold the boats, issued duplicate titles, not paid off the loan and not provided additional boat titles as required by the loan agreement. Under the bankruptcy laws my client was out his money. However, the evidence was enough for the local prosecutor to indict the debtor corporation, as well as the husband and wife who were its shareholders and directors. As we go to press, the criminal proceeding has not been resolved. I do find it interesting, however, that the debtors—who are "bankrupt" and "destitute"—have posted $80,000 for bail and made significant offers of cash to have the charges withdrawn.

Checklist of Concerns

1. Intent is important in determining a fraudulent transfer. As noted earlier, prior planning will help avoid a claim of fraud. Plan your transfer early.

2. If possible, transfer property to non-family transferees. Transfers to trusted advisers and associates should be your goal since your aim is asset protection, not asset giveaways.

3. The best evidence is on paper. If you have loans or transactions with friends, support them with the right documents. In the chapter on corporations, you will learn the importance of maintaining corporate formalities. This should follow through on all of your asset dealings. Creditors will be hard pressed to overturn a properly documented exchange.

4. Show nonprotection reasons for transfers. It should be obvious that gifts are well-intentioned, not just presented to get property out of your hands and away from creditors.

5. Develop a consistent plan of gifting transfers. Make them small and they will likely be unnoticed. Consider this example: A parent has three children, and for the past five years has given each child $1,000 per year. In the sixth year, the parent is sued. The $15,000 received by the children over the previous five years is free from attack as a fraudulent transfer.

   Now, consider the parent who has *not* developed an asset protection plan. He or she has not made annual gifts. In the same year, that parent is sued and transfers $15,000 to his or her children. If the parent cannot satisfy the creditor's claim, the gift may very well be vulnerable to a claim of fraudulent transfer.

6. Know your state's statute of limitations for various claims. The statute of limitations is the law that defines when a party's right to pursue a claim has expired. Although the UFCA does not contain a specific statute of limitations, each state enacted its own time limit when it adopted the UFCA. The time to challenge or void a fraudulent conveyance ranges from three to six years, depending on your state. Should the debtor be in bankruptcy, the Bankruptcy Code establishes the federal statute of limitations. Section 548 of the Bankruptcy Code provides that "the trustee may avoid any transfer of an interest of the debtor in property. . . that was made or incurred on or within one year before the date of the filing of the petition."

Creditors have rights, too. The *law of fraudulent conveyance* was established to give a creditor the right to go after property that was moved by the debtor just to avoid collection of the debt. If a transfer is found to be fraudulent, the creditor can continue to go after both the debtor and the transferred property. In essence, this gives the creditor additional property from which to satisfy its claim.

As a rule, creditors pursue cost-effective means of collection. It can be expensive and time consuming to pursue a fraudulent transfer claim, and many creditors will back off from this expense. However, some creditors will fight on, regardless of cost. Do not delude yourself into believing a fraudulent transfer will protect your assets. For example, I had one client who was willing to pay me $500 to collect a $100 debt. He didn't care a whit about the cost; he simply would not permit a debtor to beat him.

Figure 2.1 Uniform Fraudulent Conveyance Act

Sec. 1. Definition of Terms. In this act "Assets" of a debtor means property not exempt from liability for his debts. To the extent that any property is liable for any debts of the debtor, such property shall be included in his assets.

"Conveyance" includes every payment of money, assignment, release, transfer, lease, mortgage or pledge of tangible or intangible property, and also the creation of any lien or encumbrance.

"Creditor" is a person having any claim, whether matured or unmatured, liquidated or unliquidated, absolute, fixed or contingent.

"Debt" includes any legal liability, whether matured or unmatured, liquidated or unliquidated, absolute, fixed or contingent.

Sec. 2. Insolvency.

(1) A person is insolvent when the present fair salable value of his assets is less than the amount that will be required to pay his probable liability on his existing debts as they become absolute and matured.

(2) In determining whether a partnership is insolvent there shall be added to the partnership property the present fair salable value of the separate assets of each general partner in excess of the amount probably sufficient to meet the claims of his separate creditors, and also the amount of any unpaid subscription to the partnership of each limited partner, provided the present fair salable value of the assets of such limited partner is probably sufficient to pay his debts, including such unpaid subscription.

Sec. 3. Fair Consideration. Fair consideration if given for property, or obligation,

(a) When in exchange for such property, or obligation, as a fair equivalent therefor, and in good faith, property is conveyed or a previous debt is satisfied, or

(b) When such property, or obligation is received in good faith to secure a present advance or antecedent debt in amount not disproportionately small as compared with the value of the property, or obligation obtained.

Sec. 4. Conveyances by Insolvent. Every conveyance made and every obligation incurred by a person who is or will be thereby rendered insolvent is fraudulent as to creditors without regard to his actual intent if the conveyance is made or the obligation is incurred without a fair consideration.

Sec. 5. Conveyances by Persons in Business. Every conveyance made without fair consideration when the person making it is engaged or is about to engage in a business or transaction for which the property remaining in his hands after the conveyance is an unreasonably small capital, is fraudulent as to creditors and as to other persons who become creditors during the continuance of such business or transaction without regard to his actual intent.

Figure 2.1   Uniform Fraudulent Conveyance Act (Continued)

Sec. 6. Conveyances by a Person about to Incur Debts. Every conveyance made and every obligation incurred without fair consideration when the person making the conveyance or entering into the obligation intends or believes that he will incur debts beyond his ability to pay as they mature, is fraudulent as to both present and future creditors.

Sec. 7. Conveyance Made with Intent to Defraud. Every conveyance made and every obligation incurred without fair consideration when the person making the conveyance or entering into the obligation intends or believes that he will incur debts beyond his ability to pay as they mature, is fraudulent as to both present and future creditors.

Sec. 8. Conveyance of Partnership Property. Every conveyance of partnership property and every partnership obligation incurred when the partnership is or will be thereby rendered insolvent, is fraudulent as to partnership creditors, if the conveyance is made or obligation is incurred

   (a) To a partner, whether with or without a promise by him to pay partnership debts, or

   (b) To a person (not a partner) without fair consideration to the partnership as distinguished from consideration to the individual partners.

Sec. 9. Rights of Creditors Whose Claims Have Matured.

(1) Where a conveyance or obligation is fraudulent as to a creditor, such creditor, when his claim has matured, may, as against any person except a purchaser for fair consideration without knowledge of the fraud at the time of the purchase, or one who has derived title immediately from such a purchaser,

   (a) Have the conveyance set aside or obligation annulled to the extent necessary to satisfy his claim, or

   (b) Disregard the conveyance and attach or levy execution upon the property conveyed.

(2) A purchaser who without actual fraudulent intent has given less than a fair consideration for the conveyance or obligation, may retain the property or obligation as security for repayment.

Sec. 10. Rights of Creditors Whose Claims Have Not Matured. Where a conveyance made or obligation incurred is fraudulent as to a creditor whose claim has not matured he may proceed in a court of competent jurisdiction against any person against whom he could have proceeded had his claim matured, and the court may,

   (a) Restrain the defendant from disposing of his property,

   (b) Appoint a receiver to take charge of the property,

   (c) Set aside the conveyance or annul the obligation, or

   (d) Make any order which the circumstances of the case may require.

Sec. 11. Cases Not Provided For in Act. In any case not provided for in the Act the rules of law and equity including the law merchant, and in particular the rules relating to the law of principal and agent, and the effect of fraud, misrepresentation, duress or coercion, mistake, bankruptcy or other invalidating cause shall govern.

Sec. 12. Construction of Act. This Act shall be so interpreted and construed as to effectuate its general purpose to make uniform the law of those states which enact it.

Sec. 13. Name of Act. This Act may be cited as the Uniform Fraudulent Conveyance Act.

Sec. 14. Inconsistent Legislation Repealed Section .... are hereby repealed, and all acts or parts of acts inconsistent with this Act are hereby repealed.

3

Understanding and Coping with Collection Procedures

Most people who are at risk of losing their property have multiple debts, such as credit cards and installment loans. This creates an interesting tension among creditors, who in essence compete to be the first to take a debtor's property to satisfy their debt. Although many professionals and business people fear the risk posed by a lawsuit seeking catastrophic damages, most debtors are simply overextended.

We live in a society that is driven by credit. Just look at the newspaper and television advertisements offering credit opportunities. It is not surprising that the financial difficulties threatening most debtors are related to the overextension of credit.

Financial difficulties are usually the result of *borrowing too much* and not having the ability to stay current with payment obligations. If this is true in your case, it's likely that your creditors are pressuring you to pay. This pressure is probably magnified by the fact that you have many separate creditors. These creditors may pursue you with letters and phone calls that threaten to damage your credit rating, to institute a lawsuit against you or to take your property.

Asset protection provides early intervention in order to alleviate this stress. You must know what your creditors are allowed to do in order to develop the most appropriate plan. The purpose of any plan is to:

- eliminate or lessen the stress;
- protect your property from loss;
- restructure your payments to levels you can afford; or
- give you a breathing period during which you can protect your assets.

Creditor Collection Techniques

Creditors are not the bad guys in black hats. They are business people, many of whom are located in your community. They are in business to make money. It is their primary goal to sell and hopefully develop goodwill with you as their customer. Remember the motto, "the customer is always right." Creditors will work with you if they believe that you are acting in good faith, not just stringing them along. Your continued business and your goodwill are more important than what they might lose if they act inappropriately.

Keep in mind that collection is a cost of business and must be economical. It makes little sense for a business to spend an additional 50 cents to collect a dollar. Many creditors will, after a modest effort to collect a small account receivable, write it off. It does not benefit them to continue to pursue small sums of money. As ironic as it may seem, your small account gives you more clout in compromising the overdue portion of your debt than you would have if you owed a large amount of money.

What are the steps a creditor will take to collect accounts? Usually the first step is the bill itself. Thereafter, you will receive reminder statements. Initially the reminder will be a mild notice that your payment is late. It is written to give the impression that your creditor has assumed that you have only overlooked a late payment. In actuality, it is initiated by a computer that generates notices simply by reference to fixed "cutoff" dates. Those accounts that have not yet made a timely payment automatically receive notice. These notices usually will prompt payment. Sometimes it may take a second or third reminder, but most people will pay up.

After the second or third reminder goes unanswered, credit departments take notice and begin to act. When the third reminder goes out, the payment in question is probably 90 days overdue. Creditors recognize that the longer they delay in pursuing collection, the less chance they have of collecting. At this point you may be receiving notices on a weekly basis. From the creditor's viewpoint, it is important to let you know that they have not overlooked your debt.

If these notices prove ineffective, the creditor's collection department may write or call to ask you if there are any problems. Again, this is an inoffensive contact used to show your creditor's concern. With the advent of computerized voice-mail, the telephone call is becoming the contact of choice. It is relatively inexpensive, fast and efficient.

Many credit card companies will use the information they receive during a call to you to judge whether it has become appropriate to cancel your credit card. Remember, credit card companies, such as Visa and MasterCard, provide no product; they make their money like banks, on the fees they collect. If they decide you are a bad risk, they will cancel your card in order to limit their exposure.

It is important that you recognize the full importance of the initial phone call from a creditor, particularly a credit card company. Creditors use this call to obtain information that will help them decide whether they can expect payment from you or whether they should turn the account over to a collection agency.

Once your creditors enlist a collection agency, they are no longer concerned about your goodwill or your continued patronage. To the contrary, they only want to cut their losses and receive the maximum they can from you. Your best strategy, even in difficult times, is to try to keep your account from going to a collection agency. In fact, your telephone contact may even tell you that they will not refer the matter to a credit reporting agency if you can make some other arrangement.

If one of your problems involves credit card debt, consider that many credit card issuers will work with you to avoid referring your account to collection. Often, credit card issuers will reduce the minimum monthly payment to less than the regular monthly minimum shown on your bill.

What Collection Agencies Do

Once your account has been referred to a collection agency, a new process begins. You will receive a letter from the agency advising you that they have been retained to collect your debt. The letter will notify you to contact the agency, tell you how much money you owe and to whom you owe it. Under the terms of the Fair Debt Collection Act (FDCA), the letter will provide you with an opportunity to contest the amount owed. Although it is not a frequent event, collection departments do make errors and this is your last chance to correct the record. The reputation for toughness that most collection agencies enjoy convinces many people to pay their debt after receiving the first letter.

After the initial contact, the collection agency will be more aggressive than your creditor in trying to collect the debt. The collection agency is in business to make money, and it only makes money by collecting debts.

Typically, collection agencies work on contingency. In other words, they are paid on a percentage of the amount collected. This percentage may be as high as 40 percent or 50 percent of the amount collected. Remember, by the time the account has been sent to the collection agency, your creditor has written off your debt and any proceeds it may receive will be viewed as "found money."

Collection agencies have become very efficient. As with your creditor, their initial contacts may be cordial reminders of your legal and moral obligation to pay. Thereafter, the collection agency will be more forceful and threatening in tone. The frequency of contact and the intimidating nature of the contacts will increase exponentially.

Many collection agencies prefer, after the initial contact letter, to proceed over the telephone. The telephone provides them with the advantages of intimidation and flexibility in exaggerating—factors that may not be "legal." It is easy for you simply to ignore a letter, but many people are frightened by a voice at the other end of the line. Additionally, it is easier to embarrass a debtor during a telephone call than it is in a letter. At some point, the collection agency will determine whether they can expect you to pay. If the decision goes against you, they will refer the matter to an attorney for legal action. You may even receive a letter demanding payment and warning you that this will be your last opportunity to pay before the matter is referred to an attorney.

Once an attorney has been retained, the process will begin again. Many collection attorneys will initially try to resolve the matter by negotiating a settlement for a reduced amount. Like the collection agency, the attorney is paid only for successful collection efforts. Today, attorneys are more aggressive and often proceed directly to court. Should you be sued, immediately seek legal advice. If you ignore the suit, your creditor will obtain a judgment against you.

How the Law Limits Collection Practices

The Fair Debt Collection Practices Act prohibits debt collectors from the following:

- Communicating with you "at any unusual time or place or a time or place known or which should be known to be inconvenient to the consumer." In the absence of knowledge of circumstances to the contrary, debt collectors must assume that convenient times are limited to the hours between 8 A.M. and 9 P.M.
- Communicating with you at your place of employment if the debt collector knows or has reason to know that your employer prohibits employees from receiving such communications.
- Continuing to contact you after receiving written notification from you that you wish the debt collector to stop contacting you. In that situation, debt collectors may only:
  - contact you to say that their efforts to collect have ended;
  - notify you that specific remedies may be pursued; and,
  - notify you that a specific remedy is being pursued.
- Contacting you or others, if they know that you are represented by an attorney.
- Communicating your debt to someone other than you, the creditor, your attorney or a credit reporting agency.

The FDCPA specifically addresses the issue of harassment and abuse. Section 1692d provides:

> A debt collector may not engage in any conduct the natural consequence of which is to harass, oppress, or abuse any person in connection with the collection of a debt. Without limiting the general application of the foregoing, the following conduct is a violation of this section:
>
> (1) The use or threat of use of violence or other criminal means to harm the physical person, reputation, or property of any person.
> (2) The use of obscene or profane language or language the natural consequence of which is to abuse the hearer or reader.
> (3) The publication of a list of consumers who allegedly refuse to pay debts, except to a consumer reporting agency....
> (4) The advertisement for sale of any debt to coerce payment of the debt.

(5) Causing a telephone to ring or engaging any person in telephone conversation repeatedly or continuously with intent to annoy, abuse, or harass any person at the called number.

(6) . . .the placement of telephone calls without meaningful disclosure of the caller's identity.

The FDCPA defines conduct constituting unfair practices as follows:

- Accepting a check post-dated more than five days without written notification to you of their intention to deposit the check. The check may not be deposited with less than three days nor more than ten days written notice to you. (The purpose of this provision is to give you the opportunity to ensure that there are sufficient funds in your checking account when the check is eventually deposited.)

- Soliciting a post-dated check for the purpose of threatening criminal prosecution.

- Depositing or threatening to deposit any post-dated check prior to the date on the check.

- Communicating with a consumer regarding a debt by postcard. (This is to ensure your privacy.)

- Concealing the true purpose of a collect telephone call or collect telegram in order to get you to accept the call or telegram and pay the charges.

- Using any language or symbol, other than the debt collector's address, on any envelope or telegram if that language or symbol would indicate the correspondence is from a debt collector. (The debt collector may not even use its business name on the envelope if its name would identify it as a debt collector.)

The FDCPA defines false or misleading practices as follows:

A debt collector may not use any false, deceptive, or misleading representation or means in connection with the collection of any debt. Without limiting the general application of the foregoing, the following conduct is a violation of this section:

(1) The false representation or implication that the debt collector is vouched for, bonded by, or affiliated with the United States or any State, including the use of any badge, uniform, or facsimile thereof.

(2) The false representation of–
   (A) the character, amount , or legal status of any debt; or
   (B) any services rendered or compensation which may be lawfully received by any debt collector for the collection of a debt.

(3) The false representation or implication that any individual is an attorney or that any communication is from an attorney.

(4) The representation or implication that nonpayment of any debt will result in the arrest or imprisonment of any person or the seizure, garnishment, attachment, or sale of any property or wages of any person unless such action is lawful and the debt collector or creditor intends to take such action.

(5) The threat to take any action that cannot legally be taken or that is not intended to be taken.

(6) The false representation or implication that a sale, referral, or other transfer of any interest in a debt shall cause the consumer to–
(A) lose any claim or defense to payment of the debt, or
(B) become the subject to any practice prohibited by this subchapter.

(7) The false representation or implication that the consumer committed any crime or other conduct in order to disgrace the consumer.

(8) Communicating or threatening to communicate to any person credit information which is known or which should be known to be false, including the failure to communicate that a disputed debt is disputed.

(9) The use or distribution of any written communication which simulates or is falsely represented to be a document authorized, issued, or approved by any court, official, or agency of the United States, or any State, or which creates a false impression as to its source, authorization, or approval.

(10) The use of any false representation or deceptive means to collect or attempt to collect any debt or to obtain information concerning a consumer.

(11) Except as otherwise provided for communications to acquire location information under section 1692b of this title, the failure to disclose clearly in all communications made to collect a debt, or to obtain information about a consumer, that the debt collector is attempting to collect a debt and that any information obtained will be used for that purpose.

(12) The false representation or implication that accounts have been turned over to innocent purchasers for value.

(13) The false representation or implication that documents are legal process.

(14) The use of any business, company, or organization name other than the true name of the debt collector's business, company or organization.

(15) The false representation or implication that documents are not legal process forms or do not require legal action by the consumer.

(16) The false representation or implication that a debt collector operates or is employed by a consumer reporting agency as defined by section 1681a(f) of this title.

If you are faced with what you believe to be a "harassing" collection agency, you can halt their efforts by complaining to the Federal Trade Commission or your state's consumer protection agency. Should you determine that the collector has broken the law, you may now have an effective weapon against the collection effort. The collector's violations of the FDCPA may even entitle you to monetary damages. It would be poetic justice if, in effect, the collection company paid your bill.

Debt Resolution Without Bankruptcy

Assume that your debts exceed your income, or at least your ability to provide for your family's bare necessities if you paid all of your obligations. Collection agencies are likely to be telephoning you, and you have been threatened with losing everything you own. Something has to give. Ultimately you can resolve many of these claims by declaring bankruptcy, but, for a number of reasons, bankruptcy should be a course of last resort. Instead, you should consider the potential of bankruptcy as a tool with which you can get your creditors to listen to reason. They know full well that if you do go into bankruptcy, they are unlikely to get more than a few cents of every dollar you owe.

By gently reminding your creditors that you are contemplating bankruptcy, they may become more willing to work with you or give you the time you need to put one or all three of the following options into play:

1. Consolidate your debts.
2. Enter into a new installment agreement.
3. Try to compromise the amount due.

In order to choose the correct strategy or combination of strategies, you need to understand your ability to borrow or make payments. First, you must measure your ability to borrow. The forms that appear at the end of this chapter should prove useful in collecting information and determining your borrowing strength. You must account for all of the cash, stocks, bonds, investments, life insurance and other property against which you can borrow—particularly real estate. If the total of your available assets is greater than your outstanding debts, you may be served by a debt consolidation loan.

There is one caution that must be posted: a consolidation loan will enable you to satisfy your current debt—but it will create a new debt that you will have to pay down. You must ensure that the monthly payments on your consolidation loan are meaningfully lower than the total of the payments the loan will satisfy. Do not dig a bigger hole by signing up for a loan that requires monthly payments greater than either your ability to repay or your current monthly payments.

Next, measure your income's ability to service your existing debts. To do this, determine your monthly income after deductions for taxes (federal, state and local income tax and social security) and other withholding items, i.e., union dues, support payments, wage garnishment, medical and/or life insurance coverage and I.R.A.s.

Now, list all of your expenses. Do not be stingy—be realistic as to what you must spend. Do not underestimate costs of food, your mortgage or rent, gasoline, telephone, utilities and clothing. In addition, make sure that you include annual and other installment obligations, such as property taxes, car insurance, school tuition, water and other utility bills that come due other than monthly. Include these obligations and "budget" a monthly amount for them. Too many debtors ignore the need to set aside this money and break their budget when the semi-annual homeowner's insurance policy premium arrives. The premium gets paid, but the debtors cannot pay the bills for the rest of their necessities for the next several weeks.

Now, subtract your monthly expenses from your *net take-home pay*. If the number is a positive number, that is your available source of funds for debt reduction. It is the money you will use to repay your overdue and delinquent bills.

If the amount is zero or less, your income alone will not resolve your problem. You should explore the possibility of obtaining a debt consolidation loan, a negotiated installment agreement or a compromise of your accounts, and, as a last resort, bankruptcy.

If your income will allow you to pay your delinquencies within a year, you have a sporting chance to reach an understanding with your creditors. You will have to be honest, both with yourself and your creditors. If you do not have the income strength to pay off your bills within one year, some compromise or bankruptcy is in order.

Many locales have consumer credit and debt counseling agencies. The best of these are not-for-profit and will provide debt counseling or act as an intermediary with your creditors in order to establish a program that you can afford. Their services are available for little or no charge. Usually these agencies are listed in your local *Yellow Pages* under the "Credit Counseling Services" heading.

Debt Consolidation Loans

A debt consolidation loan is a single, large borrowing, the proceeds of which are used to pay off a group of smaller loans. Given the nature of the lenders who offer debt consolidation loans, there is a better than average chance that the interest rate you'll have to pay them will be less than the interest rates associated with charge cards and other consumer loans. A second benefit flows from the fact that your debt consolidation loan can be stretched out over a longer term than most consumer loans, which means you will pay less to amortize the loan each month.

There is a tradeoff here. You will ultimately pay more in interest on a debt consolidation loan since it runs for a longer term than your consumer loans. But, you'll be paying less each month, and that can help you get out of a difficult situation.

Shopping for a Debt Consolidation Loan

Start with family. Although you may think it humiliating, families do tend to make an effort to protect their own. If your family members have the financial wherewithal, they may be willing to pull you out of your difficulties. Or, instead of lending the money directly to you, your family may be willing to use its cash as collateral for a loan from your credit union or bank. Loans backed by certificates of deposit, for example, receive the most favorable interest rates available.

Finance companies, often the least discriminating lenders, are another option. These companies will charge a fairly high interest rate, so you should carefully compare their monthly payment requirements to your existing payment totals.

Second, or *home equity*, loans have become popular tools for financing. The home equity loan "converts" the equity you have in your home to cash. This pool of cash may be enough for you to pay off your debts. Even if you have a bad credit history, do not be afraid to pursue a home equity loan. You'll be offering sound collateral (your home), and you may be able to get a meaningfully lower interest rate than the rate charged by finance companies.

If you are a participant in a pension plan, you may have an excellent source of capital. Find out if your pension plan was structured to allow you to borrow against it. A pension is permitted by law to loan money to participants, but does not have to do so unless the terms of the plan allow borrowing. The law permits pension plans to loan money to plan participants subject to the following provisions: you can borrow at least $10,000 and not more than $50,000; amounts between those two figures can be loaned if they do not exceed one-half of your vested account balance. The loan must be amortized regularly over the five-year period, which means that the loan payments must include both principal and interest and must be made at least quarterly. Loans may not be structured as a single payment balloon at the end of the term.

The $50,000 limit is per employer or plan sponsor, and it is a personal limit. Therefore, if you and your spouse are both members of pension plans, you could borrow up to $100,000. The $100,000 limit is not adversely affected by the fact that you and your spouse are members of the same pension plan or members of pension plans sponsored by different employers.

Review your life insurance policies. Many policies provide a *cash value* against which you can borrow. If your policy is new, this amount may be minimal. On older policies the cash surrender value may be substantial.

Your Pension Plan

If you are a participant in a 401(k) plan, you may have an additional source of money. A 401(k) plan is a type of profit sharing plan that is permitted to defer tax on income put into the plan until the money is withdrawn

A 401(k) plan is permitted to make distributions to plan participants undergoing a hardship. To qualify as a hardship, the problem must create an immediate and heavy financial burden that the withdrawal will satisfy in whole or in part. Internal Revenue regulations require the decision to make a hardship distribution be made pursuant to objective standards established by the pension plan's trustees. The decision as to whether such a need exists is made on an individual basis. IRS regulations provide five safe harbor standards under which plan distributions will qualify as hardship withdrawals:

1. Medical expenses for the plan participant, the participant's spouse, dependents, children or parents
2. Purchase of a principal residence, but not a vacation home
3. Payment of the next year's college tuition for the plan participant, the participant's spouse, children or dependents
4. Payments necessary to prevent eviction from the participant's primary residence
5. Any other events as determined by the IRS in the future (To date no other events have been added to the list.)

The regulations also govern how much you may take in a hardship distribution. Under the regulations:

> A distribution is deemed necessary to satisfy an immediate and heavy financial need of an employee if all of the following requirements are satisfied:
>
> 1. The distribution is not in excess of the amount of the immediate and heavy financial need of the employee. The amount of an immediate and heavy financial need may include any amounts necessary to pay any federal, state, or local income taxes or penalties reasonably anticipated to result from the distribution.
> 2. The employee has obtained all distributions, other than hardship distributions and all nontaxable (at the time of the loan) loans currently available under all plans maintained by the employer.
> 3. The plan and all other plans maintained by the employer limit the employee's elective contributions for the next taxable year to the applicable limit under section 402(g) for that year minus the employee's elective contributions for the year of the hardship distribution.
> 4. The employee is prohibited, under the terms of the plan or an otherwise legally enforceable agreement, from making elective contributions and employee contributions to the plan and all other plans maintained by the employer for at least 12 months after receipt of the hardship distribution. For this purpose the phrase 'all other plans maintained by the employer' means all qualified and nonqualified plans of deferred compensation maintained by the employer. The phrase includes a stock option, stock purchase, or similar plan, or a cash or deferred arrangement that is part of a cafeteria plan within the meaning of section 125. However, it does not include the mandatory employee contribution portion of a defined benefit plan. It also does not include a health or welfare benefit plan, including one that is part of a cafeteria plan within the meaning of section 125. Treas. Reg. 1.401(k)-1.

In essence you may take only the amount necessary to pay off your hardship and any related income tax consequences. You could not, for example, take a distribution and buy a new car for personal use. However, you could pay for the funeral of a family member or a set of braces for a child's teeth. One negative consequence of a hardship withdrawal is that the amount of the withdrawal will be excluded from the plan for the next 12 months after the distribution.

You will be able to withdraw only your elective deferrals and the earnings on your deferrals through December 31, 1988. Although this may not seem fair, remember that these plans and their funds are intended to be used for retirement purposes and not as bank accounts.

Selling Assets to Raise Money

You may choose to sell some of your belongings to raise money. If so, try to follow these rules:

- Be realistic in determining the value of your property. Your "customers" know they are not shopping in a store that handles new merchandise, and they may suspect that you are selling under distress.
- Try to sell property that has high value or desirability.
- Sell only items that you will not have to replace.
- Try not to be emotional, even if the property you have to put up for sale holds an emotional attachment for you. The relief from the stress created by your creditors usually overcomes the sentimental attachment you have for a family heirloom.
- If possible, return property to creditors who are pressing you. Make certain to obtain a release. This will absolve you of any of the outstanding debt on the original transaction. If you do not get a release, your creditor will come after you for the difference between the amount you owed and the value of the returned property.

If these options are available to you, you should be able to work your way free from your debt problems. If you do, keep this sad fact of life in mind: Many people who are newly debt-free act like alcoholics and go back to their old habits. In no time such people are deeply in debt, but now they have fewer assets with which to work their way out of trouble. There are just so many times a house can be mortgaged.

The way to get out of debt and stay out of debt is to operate religiously within the confines of a budget. This does not mean that you have no leeway for discretionary spending. It does mean that you must be disciplined in your spending.

Develop Your Extended Payment Schedule

Assume you've done all that you can. You have sold all nonessential property, remortgaged your home and tried unsuccessfully to borrow from every conceivable source. You've come up short, and your creditors are still hounding you.

Do not despair; there are still two options to consider. Using the creditor's fear that you may file for bankruptcy protection, you may be able to get your creditors to agree to an extended repayment schedule. The benefit of extended repayment plans is that they allow you to reduce the amount of your monthly payments. If you have a regular income stream, you should try to reach an extended payment plan with your creditors. Most creditors fear bankruptcy because they know that they will generally get only pennies on the dollar. An extended plan offers creditors the chance to get full payment, albeit later than expected.

Make your plan livable. A nightmare situation can occur when you develop a plan and three months later cannot afford to continue it. You will have lost all credibility, and your creditors may force you into bankruptcy.

Let's look at an example. When Jane inherited her grandmother's home, the house was fully paid for, and Jane had no long-term debt obligations. Unfortunately, Jane ran up credit card debt and then borrowed to buy a new car. When she had trouble keeping up with all of this new debt, the creditors were willing to work with her. However, four months after Jane's attorney negotiated a payment plan, she just stopped paying. The result was predictable: Jane's car was repossessed, and the credit card companies demanded immediate payment. The tragedy is that today Jane's home—which she had owned free and clear of any lien—is now encumbered by the credit card companies' liens. If her creditors choose to foreclose on their liens, Jane will lose her home at a sheriff's sale.

The Two Types of Extended Plans

There are two forms of extended payment plans that are not within bankruptcy: *self-administered* and *credit counselor* plans.

In a self-administered approach, you contact your creditors and offer the terms with the threat of bankruptcy in the background. Many times this is enough to be successful.

I recently met with a client who owed about $10,000 in unsecured debt and wanted to declare bankruptcy. However, he had a steady job and did have about $300 a month to put toward bills. We contacted all of his creditors, which did two things. First, it took the collection agency off my client's case because he followed the FDCPA and told them to stop contacting him. Second, the creditors were notified that we were attempting in good faith to resolve my client's financial difficulties. Most creditors readily consented to a three-year repayment plan, once they recognized that they were all being treated equally. The few creditors that tried to take a hard line backed down when faced with the prospect that my client could offer no other option than filing for bankruptcy.

As discussed earlier, this approach requires you to make a realistic budget and have a firm handle on your ability to pay. In effect, you enter into a new contract with all of your creditors. Treat all of them equally, and the strategy should be successful. However, you must be able to live with your agreement, because you will not get a second chance.

The second non-bankruptcy approach calls for you to use a credit counseling service sponsored by your local consumer credit counseling service. This is a more formalized approach than the self-administered plan. Creditors favor this approach since you agree to turn your paycheck over to the credit service. The service gives you an allowance to live on and uses the rest of your paycheck to service your debt. Most creditors are willing to trust a consumer credit service to verify that your plan is fair and honest.

Both of these approaches require you to be open about your situation. At the end of this chapter, you will find a sample letter that you can use to propose an extended debt repayment plan. Look it over carefully. You will see that you should not hide your difficulties, but own up to them and rely on the good judgment of your creditor to work the problem out with you.

Here are some things to look out for:

- Make sure your arrangement is in writing. Your worst nightmare could come to life if you proceed to make payments and then suddenly end up on the receiving end of a lawsuit thrown at you by a disgruntled creditor. If the agreement is in writing, you have a contract that will protect you from such sneak attacks.

- Wait until you get all of your creditors in line. Why pay before you have an agreement with all of your creditors? You want this to be a productive arrangement. If less than all creditors eventually accept your plan, the non-consenting creditors may end up forcing you into bankruptcy.

- Make the acceptance of the program a condition to your beginning it. Require that at least 85 percent of your unsecured creditors participate. This may exert enough pressure for all of your unsecured creditors to sign up.

- If possible, do not sign away any of your legal rights. Many creditors will ask that you consent to a confession of judgment to them as part of the agreement. A confession of judgment would allow a creditor to get a judgment against you simply by filing the confession with the court. You are precluded from defending the claim. In some states this is not permissible. Check your state's laws.

Compromise the Claim

A compromise agreement usually provides the last opportunity that you and your creditors will have to resolve your debt problems short of a lawsuit or a bankruptcy filing. In effect, you are prenegotiating a bankruptcy result. You will educate your creditors to the fact that you have very little equity, so that they will understand that it will not be fruitful for them to sue you and that you are willing to give them at least what they would get if you declared bankruptcy.

A compromise requires you to be fair and equitable with your creditors. Try to provide an up-front cash payment and some form of payout with which you can live.

A compromise agreement is a contract that binds you and your creditors. A sample compromise agreement is printed at the end of this chapter. You may negotiate with any of your creditors, but unless you enlist your largest creditors, you will be unable to enlist the others. You must negotiate in good faith.

Reaching a compromise on your debts requires both you and your creditors to be flexible. Keep in mind the fact that creditors only want their money.

What Will You Offer?

Be fair, but start on the low side. Do not make your best offer—this is a horse swap, not a retail purchase. Increase your offer in modest amounts. Do not let your creditors bully you. You know that in the worst situation you can always go bankrupt.

When Should You Pay?

Offer what you can afford as an up-front payment. Do not offer more than you will have available in the future. Do not project possible increases in income when you make your offer. Work with what you are making today, since you have no guarantee that you will be earning more in the future.

How Long Should the Compromise Last?

Try not to permit the compromise agreement to set a term of more than two years. Never agree to a schedule that exceeds three years. Even bankruptcy only requires you to pay out over a three-year schedule. If faced with creditors unwilling to compromise on time, let them face you in bankruptcy. They will not get more from you in bankruptcy than through a compromise agreement, and they know that for a fact.

Should You Return Property?

Maybe. Property has value, and the basis of your debt is value. Negotiate the best exchange price, and try to get a release for the deficiency.

Should You Pay Interest on the Outstanding Balance?

Your creditors will expect interest to be paid. Often the interest charge is what got you in trouble initially. Try not to agree to pay interest. As you will see in Chapter 5, creditors do not receive interest in bankruptcy. If your creditors do not know this, educate them.

Can You Protect Your Credit Rating?

You may be able to negotiate a good record from your creditors, once you've established a track record of timely payments in conformity with your agreement. This is subject to mutual agreement, and you will probably have to push for it. But, it is worth fighting for, since it provides you with a tool to rehabilitate a bad credit history.

Your Best Selling Points

You must convince your creditors that it is in their best interest to come to an agreement with you outside of bankruptcy. Stress the following:

- Regular payments are better than no payments.
- The compromise will enable your creditors to avoid the use of a collection agency or lawyer—options that can cost up to 25 percent of the amount they collect.
- You are not a deadbeat looking to *beat* the system. You have come forward in a sincere manner at a difficult time. You are entitled to be treated with respect.
- You are trying to avoid bankruptcy. As previously stated, many bankruptcies result in less than five cents on the dollar being paid to creditors. Your creditors know this and should be willing to compromise—particularly if it appears that they will be getting more than they would in a bankruptcy. Remember, while you may be able to file for bankruptcy without a lawyer, if your creditors are corporations, they must be represented by a lawyer. Legal costs can eat up virtually all of the return that creditors receive from a bankrupt estate.

For all of the above reasons, a sensible creditor should be willing to enter into an agreement with you.

Debtor Protection Forms

The forms on the following pages can help you organize and execute your asset protection efforts.

Figure 3.1   Outstanding Debt (Include Credit Card Debt)

Creditor	Total Debt	Amount Paid	Amount Outstanding	Due Date
Mortgages				
_____	___	___	___	___
_____	___	___	___	___
Automobile Loans				
_____	___	___	___	___
_____	___	___	___	___
Credit Cards				
_____	___	___	___	___
_____	___	___	___	___
_____	___	___	___	___
Revolving Credit				
_____	___	___	___	___
_____	___	___	___	___
_____	___	___	___	___
Other Loans				
_____	___	___	___	___
_____	___	___	___	___
_____	___	___	___	___
_____	___	___	___	___
Unpaid Taxes				
_____	___	___	___	___
_____	___	___	___	___
_____	___	___	___	___
_____	___	___	___	___

Figure 3.2 Net Assets Available for Borrowing

Asset	Current Fair Market Value	Current Loans Against Asset	Net Equity
Real Property			
_____	_____	_____	_____
_____	_____	_____	_____
Automobile			
_____	_____	_____	_____
_____	_____	_____	_____
Marketable Securities			
_____	_____	_____	_____
_____	_____	_____	_____
_____	_____	_____	_____
_____	_____	_____	_____
Personal Property			
_____	_____	_____	_____
_____	_____	_____	_____
_____	_____	_____	_____
_____	_____	_____	_____
_____	_____	_____	_____
_____	_____	_____	_____
Life Insurance (Cash Surrender Value)			
_____	_____	_____	_____
_____	_____	_____	_____
_____	_____	_____	_____
_____	_____	_____	_____
_____	_____	_____	_____
_____	_____	_____	_____

Figure 3.3   Bare Necessity Schedule

                                                                  Month:

Rent/Mortgage $_____

Food $_____

Clothing $_____

Utilities (Gas, Electric, Telephone, Water) $_____

Transportation (Gas, Auto Payments,
    Public Transportation) $_____

Insurance (Auto, Life, Health, Medical) $_____

Uninsured Medical (Dental, Medicines, etc.) $_____

Educational Expenses $_____

Miscellaneous:

_____ $_____

_____ $_____

_____ $_____

_____ $_____

_____ $_____

_____ $_____

_____ $_____

Total Bare Necessity Expenses $_____

Current Income after Withholding and Deductions $_____

Amount Available for Debt Reduction: $_____
    (If Bare Necessity expenses exceed Net Income,
    enter the total as a negative number)

Figure 3.4   Proposed Debt Payment Plan

Creditor	Total Amount Owed	Current Monthly Payment	Proposed Monthly Payment
_____	$_____	$_____	$_____
_____	$_____	$_____	$_____
_____	$_____	$_____	$_____
_____	$_____	$_____	$_____
_____	$_____	$_____	$_____
_____	$_____	$_____	$_____
_____	$_____	$_____	$_____
_____	$_____	$_____	$_____
_____	$_____	$_____	$_____
_____	$_____	$_____	$_____
_____	$_____	$_____	$_____
_____	$_____	$_____	$_____
_____	$_____	$_____	$_____
_____	$_____	$_____	$_____
_____	$_____	$_____	$_____
_____	$_____	$_____	$_____
_____	$_____	$_____	$_____
_____	$_____	$_____	$_____
_____	$_____	$_____	$_____
_____	$_____	$_____	$_____
_____	$_____	$_____	$_____
_____	$_____	$_____	$_____
_____	$_____	$_____	$_____

Figure 3.5   Proposal Seeking an Out-of-Court Settlement

(Date)

Mr. John Collection
Credit Manager
Creditor Corporation
123 Market Street
Collection City, FL, 00000   Account Number:

Dear Mr. Collection:

As you may know, I have fallen behind in making my monthly payments on the above-referenced account. Quite simply, my employer closed its doors three months ago, and I have been forced to accept a new job that pays less than 75 percent of the salary I earned in my former position.

Attached to this letter you will find three schedules. The first is a schedule that sets out both my monthly budget for bare necessities and, additionally, the amount I have left from my net take-home pay after paying for those necessities. At the present time, I take home less than $100 more than the amount I need for necessities.

The second attachment lists all of my creditors, the amount owed to each and the current monthly payment I am obligated to make to each creditor. As the schedule indicates, my monthly obligations to my creditors amount to $2,100, which is well above the $100 I have available. Even if all of my creditors were willing to grant me extended payback terms, it is clear that I simply do not have enough income to offer a realistic payback program.

The third attachment lists the assets against which I can borrow. Based on that schedule, I believe that I can raise enough money to pay each of my creditors 35 percent of the money I owe them, if each creditor is willing to accept such a payment as full satisfaction of the amount owed. This offer is being made on the same terms to every creditor listed on the second attachment (entitled Outstanding Debt). If accepted by my creditors, I will begin liquidating my assets and will make payment to all of my creditors no later than (date).

I recognize only too well that I am asking my creditors to suffer a loss of 65 cents on every dollar I owe. Frankly, I have no other option. From my creditors' point of view, I believe that this proposal is more attractive than a forced bankruptcy, which would probably provide as little as pennies for each dollar owed.

If the plan I have proposed is agreeable to Creditor Corporation, please sign below under the words "Agreed and Accepted" and return the original copy of this letter.

Sincerely,

Phillip Debtor

Agreed and Accepted:

_____

Date:

Figure 3.6   Agreement Extending Debt Repayment

FOR VALUE RECEIVED, the Creditor Corporation, a corporation organized under the laws of the State of Delaware, hereinafter referred to as "Creditor," and John Debtor, hereinafter referred to as "Debtor," agree to the following:

ONE   Under the terms of an agreement dated the first day of April, 19   , Debtor owes $3,000 to Creditor.

TWO   The above mentioned $3,000 was due and payable to Creditor on the first day of June, 19   , and such payment is now 90 days overdue.

THREE   Debtor is not capable of paying the $3,000 at this time.

FOUR   In consideration of Creditor's willingness to extend the time and manner in which the debt is to be repaid, Debtor hereby agrees to make payment on the following dates and in the following amounts:

Date	Amount
October, 1, 19	$1,000
November 1, 19	$1,000
December 1, 19	$1,000

FIVE   Should Debtor fail to make any of the above extended payments on the dates shown above, he shall forfeit all of his rights under this agreement and Creditor shall be entitled to demand the entire amount outstanding on the date of the default and to proceed to collect such sum. Should Debtor default and Creditor find it necessary to employ an attorney to collect all sums outstanding after the default, Debtor agrees to pay all costs of collection, including reasonable attorney's fees.

Signed this   day of   , 19

_____

Creditor

_____

Debtor

(Corporate Seal(s) if either or both parties are corporations)

Figure 3.7   Proposal To Seek Extended Repayment Program

(Date)

Mr. John Collection
Credit Manager
Creditor Corporation
123 Market Street
Collection City, FL, 00000   Account Number:

Dear Mr. Collection:

As you may know, I have fallen behind in making my monthly payments on the above-referenced account. Quite simply, my employer closed its doors three months ago, and I have been forced to accept a new job that pays less than 75 percent of the salary I earned in my former position.

I now find myself unable to pay my various debts in a timely fashion. My current earnings will enable me to meet my obligations, but only if my various creditors are willing to extend the length of my debt by lowering the amount of my monthly payments.

In order to assist you in evaluating my request, I have included two documents as an attachment to this letter. The first attachment is a schedule that sets out both my monthly budget for bare necessities as well as the amount I have left over from my net take-home pay after paying for those necessities. At the present time, I take home $650 above the amount I need for necessities.

The second attachment lists all of my creditors, the amount owed to each, the current monthly payment I am obligated to make to each creditor, and the amount I propose to make to each creditor.

As the second schedule makes clear, I do not propose to favor any one creditor. Each would receive the same percentage of the $650 I have available. Under my proposal, I would make monthly payments of $35 to the Creditor Corporation.

As you review the two attachments to this letter, I am certain you will find that my proposal is being made in the best of faith. I am sincerely committed to paying my debts in full, and I know that if you will work with me, your company will be paid in full. I also know that the plan I have proposed sets out the best possible approach to my current problems. The only other option would call for my creditors to force me into bankruptcy, a course of action that would result in my creditors receiving only a few cents on the dollars I owe them.

If the plan I have proposed is agreeable to Creditor Corporation, please sign below under the words "Agreed and Accepted" and return the original copy of this letter. I will start making payments under this proposal on the first business day of the month following the date you indicate your acceptance of my proposal

Sincerely,

Phillip Debtor
Agreed and Accepted:

_____

Date:

Figure 3.8   Formal Agreement Compromising a Debt

FOR VALUE RECEIVED, the Creditor Corporation, a corporation organized under the laws of the State of Delaware, hereinafter referred to as "Creditor" and John Debtor, hereinafter referred to as "Debtor," agree to the following:

ONE   Under the terms of an agreement dated the first day of April, 19   , Debtor owes $3,000 to Creditor.

TWO   The above mentioned $3,000 was due and payable to Creditor on the first day of June, 19   , and such payment is now 90 days overdue.

THREE   Debtor is not capable of paying the $3,000 at this time.

FOUR   In consideration of Creditor's willingness to accept a total of $1,500 in full satisfaction of the $3,000 owed by Debtor, Debtor hereby agrees to make three payments of $500 each on the following dates:

October 1, 19

November 1, 19

December 1, 19

FIVE   Should Debtor fail to make any of the above payments on the dates shown above, he shall forfeit all of his rights under this agreement and Creditor shall be entitled to demand the entire $3,000 that was outstanding prior to the date of this agreement less any payments made by Debtor subsequent to the signing of this agreement. Should Debtor default and Creditor find it necessary to employ an attorney to collect all sums outstanding after the default, Debtor agrees to pay all costs of collection, including reasonable attorney's fees.

Signed this   day of   , 19

_____

Creditor

_____

Debtor

(Corporate Seal(s) if either or both parties are corporations)

4

Secured Liens, Repossession and IRS Tax Seizures

Dealing with Secured Creditors

The creditor with the strongest claim against you is your secured creditor, e.g., the bank that holds the mortgage on your home or the lender who has a lien against the title of your car. The strength of these creditors comes from the fact that, by virtue of their secured interest, they already have a hook into your property—at least the part that is secured. Delinquency on these obligations can more quickly result in your losing the property that secures the loan. Look at all of the banks and savings and loans that are being taken over by the government. New regulations require lending institutions to act more quickly when a debtor defaults on a loan. As a result, it is more difficult to negotiate a problem loan.

Lenders actually do not want to foreclose on property. Banks are not in the real estate business. More often than not, a bank loses money when it forecloses on a parcel of property. The rash of failed banks can be traced in large part to the issuance of loans that went bad, with the result that banks ended up with non-income producing property. Remember, banks are in the business of making money by loaning money; they are not in the business of brokering real estate or, even worse, becoming landlords.

Additionally, banks do not want to show their shareholders that they are poor judges of credit. Loans on which they must foreclose hurt their financial performance and sometimes cause bank officers to lose their jobs.

Just because the lender may not want to foreclose does not mean it will not do so. The bank's position is as "protected" as possible by virtue of the fact that it is a secured creditor. You must deal with the bank on its terms. However, if the lender is not unreasonable, your good faith effort, coupled with an open and frank disclosure of your situation, may turn your lender around and give it a basis upon which to work with you instead of against you.

The Threat of Foreclosure

If you are in arrears in your mortgage, both you and the bank know it. Typically you receive monthly notices if your mortgage payment is late. If you go two or three months without a payment, you will receive both late notices and telephone calls from the bank's customer service department. *Do not ignore these calls.* Responding to them in an effective way will be the first line of defense in your efforts to avoid foreclosure. It is at this time that you will have your first opportunity to negotiate and hold off any formal foreclosure proceedings.

This first attempt at collection by the bank will give you a chance to explain your plight. For example, you may have recently been laid off. Often the bank is understanding and may agree to pursue one or more of the following alternatives:

- *Check your spending habits.* The first payment that should be made—after food—is your mortgage payment. Many people get into difficulty by spending on non-necessities. While it may call for belt tightening and may make some unsecured creditors unhappy, paying your mortgage will protect both your family and your most important asset—your home.

- *Provide a moratorium on payments for a short while.* In essence, the bank is delaying the payment obligation while you get your financial situation improved. This is generally a short-term stoppage of payments and requires you to demonstrate to the bank's satisfaction that there is enough value in your home to justify a moratorium.

- *Arrange to pay only interest.* Again, this is a short-term option, one that will run no more than six months and generally does not require the bank to make sure that there is sufficient equity. The payment of interest provides a benefit to the bank—it can at least show income on the loan. A nonperforming loan looks far worse on the bank's financial reports than a loan that makes regular interest payments. While this strategy can save you some money, be careful. The payments on newer mortgages are mostly interest, so the savings may be minor. If your mortgage is older, most of the payments will reduce the outstanding principal. You are more likely to get an interest-only plan if your mortgage is newer. You might have better luck renegotiating an older mortgage, since you will have more equity in the property if you've been paying down the mortgage for a number of years.

If none of these alternatives proves viable, do not wait. Seek out the services of an attorney who specializes in either real estate or bankruptcy. If your lawyer negotiates on your behalf before formal foreclosure proceedings begin, he or she may be able to turn the bank around, particularly if the bank did not believe you or have faith in your promises.

Some alternatives that may be successful prior to a foreclosure being completed are:

- *Refinance your current mortgage.* Since the early 1980s, mortgage rates have fluctuated and have been rising in recent years. Your problems might stem from a high mortgage rate. My first rate was 11.4 percent. I successfully refinanced at 9.5 percent and reduced my monthly payments by more than $300. This is not always an easy route to follow. Your credit might have been damaged already to the point where you cannot refinance for any savings. However, without trying you will already have lost!

- *Obtain a home equity loan.* Also known as a second mortgage, a home equity loan may provide you with the flexibility you need to catch up on your first mortgage. As noted with the payment moratorium, you must have enough value in your home to get such a mortgage. In general, a second mortgage company will lend up to 75 percent or 80 percent of the value of your home minus the already outstanding mortgage.

Tip _____

Beware! *A second mortgage is also a secured loan. Do not fall into the trap of repairing the first mortgage and falling behind on the second mortgage. If you fall into arrears on the second mortgage, you could lose your home—the second mortgagee can also foreclose when you do not meet your payment obligations. When this happens, you will only have delayed the situation instead of correcting it.*

_____

- *Change your interest rate.* This is similar to refinancing your mortgage. If you have an old mortgage, many banks would prefer to *mark up* the interest rate to current market rates. The resetting of your interest rate will probably cost you less than refinancing and may make the bank more willing to see you through a short-term difficulty.

- *Offer an "equity" interest.* This calls for you to offer to make the bank a partner in the value of your home. Not only will you make payments to the bank, but when you sell the property they will receive a percentage of the proceeds—over and above the outstanding mortgage amount. This option is generally used in the context of commercial real estate, but you may be able to convince the bank to adopt it for residential real estate.

- *Convert to negative amortization.* This strategy adds any unpaid amounts to the balance that will be owed at the end of the mortgage term. Many variable rate mortgages contain a negative amortization provision.

- *If you are elderly, consider a negative mortgage.* Similar to a negative amortization, a negative mortgage pays you monthly, and the bank recoups its loan to you when you die and your house is sold. This is generally only a good idea for elderly people who NEED the income, not to protect the house from foreclosure.

What if your situation is desperate, and the bank will not accept any of the above options? Consider the following:

- *Collateralize your loan with more property.* If you have any other property of value, offer it as additional collateral. This may give you enough *equity* in property to successfully renegotiate or refinance your mortgage.

- *Get a cosigner/guarantor.* If your credit is not strong enough, maybe the additional strength of a cosigner/guarantor will get you past the bank's objections. In effect, your cosigner is on the hook if you default. It is therefore important that you have a strong relationship with whomever you approach to cosign/guarantee for you.

- *Consider moving.* Before foreclosure, you own your home. The bank only has a lien against it for the value of the mortgage. If you cannot pay the mortgage, you may be in over your head. Selling—even in a bad market—will bring you more money than you will get if the bank forecloses. Forced sales always result in depressed prices.

- *Have your attorney carefully review your loan agreements.* Although it is likely that the agreement was properly drafted, an error can give you quite a bit of leverage. Many states have usury laws. If a loan is deemed *usurious*, the lender will not be able to collect any payment and may ultimately be responsible to you for penalties. For example, I am aware of a New Jersey situation in which the bank was forced to provide a loan below prime rate due to a drafting error in the mortgage.

- *Consider bankruptcy.* Once an individual files for bankruptcy, a foreclosure cannot proceed without bankruptcy court approval. Bankruptcy can provide you with the time you need to catch up. See Chapter 5 for a fuller explanation of why bankruptcy is a valuable option that you should not overlook, particularly if you believe—incorrectly—that persons who file for bankruptcy are stigmatized.

One final word—if you fall behind, the day is not lost. If you act promptly and maintain open lines of communication with your lender, you are more likely to succeed than you are to fail in your efforts to save your home.

Protecting Other Property

It should not surprise you to learn that creditors use the same strategies to collect debts for personal property that they employ in connection with secured property. Creditors know that a delinquent debt becomes a questionable collection the longer it goes unpaid. As a result, in today's economy collection agencies and departments move quickly to collect past due debts.

Banks and finance companies frequently subscribe to credit bureaus to keep track of clients who may be poor payers. When your payments are late, credit bureaus make this information known to their subscribers. Secured creditors usually concern themselves only with your payment on their property and the equity they have in the property. This is changing with all of the bankruptcies today. Many creditors will act swiftly to reduce their losses and may contact you more quickly about late payments than they did in the past.

As I advised with respect to mortgage problems, one option open to you is to refinance your loan. Many finance companies will offer this opportunity to *catch up*. Be careful! The only concerns finance companies have is making money. Such companies will look to your ability to pay and whether you have enough value in your property to protect their interests. If you decide to refinance, make sure that you are not just digging a deeper hole by agreeing to a monthly payment you cannot make.

As discussed earlier, communication is the key. The better you keep your creditors advised of your situation and the more good faith you show in paying the debt, the more receptive they will be to working out a new payment program. If you show some attempt to make payments—even as low as $25 a month—you can keep some of your creditors off your back.

Many of the strategies discussed above can be successful in working out your difficulties with creditors of personal property purchases.

If you are unsuccessful in negotiating a payout, you may be faced with the threat of having your property repossessed. In most states repossession is regulated by the Uniform Commercial Code (UCC), which provides the following for repossessions that are not ordered by a court:

- Creditors may repossess property without court approval if it can be done in a peaceful fashion. Car repossessors can take your car faster than a thief. Under the provision of the UCC, car repossessors will take your car in situations that fall just short of armed robbery. Do not be surprised if you go shopping and come out of the store to find that your car has disappeared.

- You are entitled to any profit on the sale of your property. Let's assume that your car was repossessed. If your loan was for $5,000 and the sale of the car was for $7,000, the finance company must give you $2,000 minus the cost of the repossession and sale. This is often more cold comfort than actual result since forced sales rarely bring the true value of an item. More often than not, the debtor is left without a car and without any income from the sale.

- You have the right to *redeem* your property by paying the full amount due on the loan plus expenses of repossession. This is all your creditor really wants. Most finance companies and banks are not in the car or boat or secured property business. Often they lose money when they have to sell property to satisfy a debt.

The UCC requires a debtor to sell repossessed property at a reasonable sale price. If your property is sold at a *commercially unreasonable* price, you may be able to sue the creditor and receive monetary damages. This is not an easy task, since you must show that the creditor did not act in good faith. Remember, you are the person who did not make timely payments of your bills, and it will not be hard for the creditor to paint you as the *bad guy*.

The IRS—Your Toughest Creditor

The tools available to the IRS are coveted by all other debt collectors. As tough as most collection agencies seem, the IRS can get even tougher. The IRS has the ability, without court action, to seize and take your property to satisfy a tax obligation. The most used tool the IRS has is the *seizure right*, which means that without prior notice to you they can grab your bank accounts and freeze them. Imagine what would happen if you started bouncing checks all over town because the IRS has seized your bank account! Seizure is also the IRS's tool of last resort. The primary strategy you should employ to prevent the IRS from seizing your property must involve a combination of cooperation and communication.

A seizure often results from a taxpayer's refusal to respond or cooperate with the IRS. This may be through ignorance or lack of understanding of the severity of the IRS's collection activities. IF YOU RECEIVE COMMUNICATION FROM THE INTERNAL REVENUE SERVICE, IT IS IMPORTANT THAT YOU PROMPTLY RESPOND AND KEEP A RECORD OF YOUR RESPONSE.

The Internal Revenue Code created a system of voluntary compliance for the payment of taxes. The *Internal Revenue Manual* provides the procedures a collection agent must comply with before acting to seize your property.

The IRS Seizure Procedure

As with all creditors, communication is the key to avoiding a seizure of property by the IRS. Although particularly receptive to requests to work out an arrangement, the IRS can't agree to a workout unless you speak with them. A quick response to an IRS letter is likely to stop a seizure from occurring.

The first step in the IRS collection process calls for the Service to send you computer-generated bills and notices. Tough collection does not occur until you hear from a collection agent or receive a *Past Due Final Notice* bill from the IRS. Prompt action and response will stop this from occurring.

The IRS has been charged to give you every reasonable chance to pay your taxes. In fact, the *Internal Revenue Manual* states, "Procedures are designed (except in jeopardy cases) to give taxpayers a reasonable chance to settle their tax liabilities voluntarily before the more drastic enforcement actions are started." [IRM 5311(3)]

The Internal Revenue Code mandates that notice of intent to seize or levy be delivered in person, at your home, place of business or by registered mail to your last *known* address. Section 6331 of the Internal Revenue Code directs that the "Past Due Final Notice" be sent prior to seizing your accounts or garnishing your wages. This notice will state that if you do not pay within ten days, the Internal Revenue Service will begin collection action.

Tip ——————————————————————————————————

Do not believe that if you do not receive the notice that the IRS cannot proceed. A mailing to your last known address satisfies the Service's good faith requirement. It is your obligation to notify the IRS of a change of address. This is normally done by changing your address on your next tax return. If you are someone who does not file tax returns, you will not be protected should the IRS fail to track you down. To the contrary, the IRS's seizure is likely to be considered valid.

The next step usually involves a call from a collection agent. This will not always occur—particularly if your debt is small. Like other collection agencies, the IRS collection agent will take a tough line with you to get you either to pay up or at least enter into a payment plan. Do not take this matter lightly. Your response to the agent at this point will dictate how the IRS proceeds against you—harshly or cooperatively.

Seizing your bank accounts or garnishing your wages is comparatively easy for the IRS and is usually the first attack used by the collection agent. The IRS can initiate action by filing a Notice of Levy with your bank or your employer. The IRS then has your undivided attention—particularly when you bounce a check or get less on payday.

It is a bit more complicated for the IRS to take other property. First, the collection officer must decide to seize property in order to satisfy the tax obligation. As mentioned earlier, your willingness to cooperate shapes the collection officer's thinking. At this point, you are inventory in the collection officer's files. The IRS likes to move inventory. If you are uncooperative, the Service will move swiftly to move you, i.e., a seizure. But, if the collection officer believes that you are acting in good faith, he or she is likely to grant an extension in order to work out a payment program—even one that compromises your bill.

If the collection officer decides to seize, he or she will determine which property should be taken. The IRS's policy is not to take property if your equity in it will not generate enough proceeds to cover the costs of the sale. All other property that is not exempt from attachment is likely to be seized or levied against.

How is equity determined? Just take the expected sale price and subtract any secured amounts you owe against the property. The best example is your home. If you owe

$80,000 in mortgages and your home is worth $120,000, your equity is $40,000. Similarly, if you owe $7,500 on your car and it is now worth $5,000, you have negative equity of $2,500. In this illustration the IRS would levy against your home but not your car, since the car would not bring in enough to cover the costs of the sale.

Recovering Your Property after an IRS Seizure

There are various ways to have your seized property returned to you. The quickest, but not the least painful, is to pay the tax liability in full. Also, the IRS must return your property once the tax liability becomes unenforceable. Other avenues for release are discretionary with the IRS personnel.

Section 6343 of the Internal Revenue Code authorizes the release of property to the taxpayer if "release of such levy will facilitate the collection of such liability." The regulations issued by the Secretary provide the following conditions of release:

> [T]he district director may release the levy as authorized under subparagraph (1) of this paragraph, if:
>
>   (i) Escrow arrangement. The delinquent taxpayer offers a satisfactory arrangement, which is accepted by the district director, for placing property in escrow to secure the payment of the liability (including expenses of levy) which is the basis of the levy. [This is usually done with either stocks and bonds or business property. It requires you to place the property in the hands of an independent party who "protects" the IRS's interest while allowing you the benefit and use of the property.]
>
>   (ii) Bond. The delinquent taxpayer delivers an acceptable bond to the district director conditioned upon the payment of the liability (including expenses of levy) which is the basis of the levy. Such bond shall be in the form provided in Section 7101 and Section 301.7101-1.
>
>   (iii) Payment of amount of United States' interest in the property. There is paid to the district director an amount determined by him to be equal to the interest of the United States in the seized property or the part of the seized property to be released." [This requires either the payment of the bill in full or entering into an installment payment plan.]
>
>   (iv) Assignment of salaries and wages. The delinquent taxpayer executes an agreement directing his employer to pay to the district director amounts deducted from the employee's wages on a regular, continuing, or periodic basis, in such manner and in such amount as is agreed upon with the district director, until the full amount of the liability is satisfied, and such agreement is accepted by the employer. [This is little more than a negotiated garnishment of your paycheck.]

(v) Installment Payment arrangement. The delinquent taxpayer makes satisfactory arrangements with the district director to pay the amount of liability in installments.

(vi) Extension of statute of limitations. The delinquent taxpayer executes an agreement to extend the statute of limitations in accordance with Section 6502(a)(2) and Regulation 301.6502-1.

(vii) Release where the value of interest of United States is insufficient to meet expenses of sale. The district director may release the levy as authorized under subparagraph (1) of this paragraph if he determines that the value of the interest of the United States in the seized property, or in the part of the seized property to be released, is insufficient to cover the expenses of the sale of such property.

Briefly looking at the different criteria for release, you can see that each one is available only at. the discretion of the IRS. Your best strategy, therefore, is to be cooperative. The best approach was already lost if you are at the point of seizure.

However, not all collection agents are unreasonable. Demonstrate good faith, and you can often get the seizure released. What is important is the demonstration of good faith. They have your property; now you must play by their rules. If you can show that but for the seizure you could get a loan to satisfy the tax liability or at least a substantial portion of it, there is an excellent chance that you will be able to get the property released.

Do not believe that just because it seized your property the IRS will go no further. The IRS will sell your property without hesitation if you do not act promptly to convince it to work with you.

Tip _____

MOST IMPORTANTLY, *do not let notices from the IRS go without attention or a response. If you are to the point of seizure, you are likely past the time to compromise or reduce the tax liability.*

_____

Can You Negotiate Your Tax Liability?

Often it is possible to reduce your payment of taxes to less than what you actually owe. The IRS has a procedure known as *Offer and Compromise*, which follows Section 5712 of the IRS Tax Collection Guidelines.

The IRS will not approach you for offer and compromise. Quite simply, they will not volunteer to "bid against" themselves, but they will entertain such an offer.

As in the case of bankruptcy (see Chapter 5), the IRS will determine what your equity is and will require you to offer at least what they would receive had they levied or seized your property. The IRS is not required to accept offers in compromise, so your good faith is a prerequisite. For example, a client of mine was advised by his accountant to make an offer of $1. This was determined by the Collection Officer and his manager to be a bad faith offer. Thereafter, it took approximately five years to rehabilitate my client's credibility in order to satisfy his tax liability. Ultimately, he was unable to reduce his liability, although some penalties were reduced.

The offer in compromise is submitted on Form 656. The form calls for you to (1) describe the violation of tax law or failure to meet a tax obligation that gave rise to the government's claim or charge against you, (2) make an offer in compromise of that claim, and (3) show your total liability (tax, interest, and penalties) for each tax period in question.

An offer of a sum of money to satisfy the tax is simply a request that the offer be accepted in compromise of your liability. The offer must include a check for the full amount you are prepared to offer.

Your offer should reflect your ability to pay. If you have assets in excess of the amount of the offer, it is unlikely that the offer will be accepted. However, if you offer all of your *net value,* and it is still less than the outstanding tax debt, the IRS may well accept your offer—even if you have the potential to pay the entire amount in the future.

Tip

CAUTION: *Do not make a compromise offer to the IRS without advice from an experienced tax professional. Although it is true that the tendered amount will be returned to you if the offer is not accepted, the IRS collection agent is likely to turn around and immediately levy on the tendered amount. That means you will have lost the money with which you hoped to compromise the claim without receiving a quid pro quo for the Internal Revenue Service.*

Figure 4.1 Statement of Financial Condition and Other Information

Form **433**
(Rev. Feb. 1982)

Statement of Financial Condition and Other Information

(Please file in duplicate with offer in compromise)

Please furnish the information requested in this form with your offer in compromise, if the offer is based in whole or in part on inability to pay the liability. If you need help in preparing this statement, call on any Internal Revenue office. It is important that you answer all questions. If a question does not apply, please enter N/A. This will speed up consideration of your offer.

1a. Name(s) of Taxpayer(s)	b. Social Security Number	c. Employer Identification Number

d. Business Address	e. Bus. Tel. No.	2. Name and Address of Representative, if any

f. Home Address	g. Home Tel. No.	

3. Kind of tax involved	Taxable period	Amount due	Amount offered
a.			
b.			
c.			
d.			
e.			

4. Due and unpaid Federal taxes, *(except those covered by this offer in compromise)*

Kind of tax	Taxable period	Amount due
a.		
b.		
c.		

5. Names of banks and other financial institutions you have done business with at any time during past 3 years—

Name and address	Name and address
a.	b.
c.	d.

e. Do you rent a safety deposit box in your name or in any other name?
☐ No   ☐ Yes *(If yes, give name and address of bank)*

6. If income withholding or employment tax is involved, please complete 6a through f

a. Were the employees' income withholding or employment taxes, due from employees on wages they received from employment, deducted or withheld from the wages paid during any period shown above?   ☐ Yes   ☐ No

b. If so, was the tax paid or deposited to the Internal Revenue Service? ☐ No ☐ Yes	c. If deducted but not paid or deposited to IRS, how did you dispose of the deducted amounts?

d. Has business in which you incurred such taxes been discontinued? ☐ No ☐ Yes	e. If so, on what date was it discontinued?

f. How did you dispose of assets of discontinued business?

7. Offer filed by individual

a. Name of Spouse	b. Age of Spouse	c. Age of Taxpayer

d. Names of dependent children or relatives	Relationship	Age
(1)		
(2)		
(3)		
(4)		
(5)		
(6)		
(7)		

Form 433 (Rev. 2-82)

61

Figure 4.1 Statement of Financial Condition and Other Information (Continued)

Please furnish your most recent financial information. In the columns below, show the cost and fair market value of each asset you own directly or indirectly. Also show all your interests in estates, trusts, and other property rights, including contingent interests and remainders.

8.　　　　　　　　　　　　　Statement of assets and liabilities as of _____
　　　　　　　　　　　　　　　　　　　　　　　　　　　　　　(date)

a.	Assets	Cost*	Fair market value
(1)	Cash	$	
(2)	Cash surrender value of insurance *(See item 9)*		
(3)	Accounts receivable *(See item 11)*		
(4)	Notes receivable *(See item 11)*		
(5)	Merchandise inventory *(See item 12)*		
(6)	Real estate *(See item 13)*		
(7)	Furniture and fixtures *(See item 14)*		
(8)	Machinery and equipment *(See item 14)*		
(9)	Trucks and delivery equipment *(See item 15)*		
(10)	Automobiles *(See item 15)*		
(11)	Securities *(See item 16)*		
(12)			
(13)			
(14)			
(15)			
(16)			
(17)			
(18)			
(19)			
(20)			
(21)			
(22)			
(23)			
(24)			
(25)			
(26)			
(27)	**Total assets** ▶	$	$

b.	Liabilities	Amount	
(1)	Loans on insurance *(See items 9 and 10)*	$	
(2)	Accounts payable		
(3)	Notes payable		
(4)	Mortgages *(See item 13)*		
(5)	Accrued real estate taxes *(See item 13)*		
(6)	Judgments *(See item 17)*		
(7)	Reserves *(Itemize)*		
(8)			
(9)			
(10)			
(11)			
(12)			
(13)			
(14)			
(15)			
(16)			
(17)			
(18)			
(19)			
(20)			
(21)			
(22)	**Total liabilities** ▶	$	

(*Less depreciation, if any)　　　　　　　　　Page 2　　　　　　　　　Form **433** (Rev. 2-82)

62

Figure 4.1 Statement of Financial Condition and Other Information (Continued)

9.	Life insurance policies now in force with right to change beneficiary reserved							
Number of Policy	Name of Company	Amount of Policy	Present Cash Surrender Value Plus Accumulated Dividends	Policy Loan	Date Made	Automatic Premium Payments*	Date Made
a.		$	$	$		$	
b.							
c.							
d.							
e.							
f.							
g.							
h.							
i.							
j.							

Show only those made before date notice of levy was served on the insurance company.

10.	Life insurance policies assigned or pledged on indebtedness		

If any of the policies listed in item 9 are assigned or pledged on indebtedness, except with insurance companies, give the following information about each policy:

Number of Policy Assigned or Pledged	Name and Address of Pledgee or Assignee	Amount of Indebtedness	Date Pledged or Assigned
a.		$	
b.			
c.			
d.			
e.			
f.			
g.			

11.	Accounts and notes receivable			
Name	Book Value	Liquidation Value	Amount of Indebtedness if Pledged	Date Pledged
a. Accounts Receivable				
(1)	$	$	$	
(2)				
(3)				
(4)				
(5)				
(6)				
(7)				
(8)				
(9)				
(10)				
(11)				
(12) Total ►	$	$	$	
b. Notes Receivable				
(1)	$	$	$	
(2)				
(3)				
(4)				
(5)				
(6)				
(7)				
(8)				
(9)				
(10)				
(11) Total ►	$	$	$	

Form 433 (Rev. 2-82)

Figure 4.1 Statement of Financial Condition and Other Information (Continued)

12. Merchandise inventory

Description	Cost	Fair Market Value	Liquidation Value	Amount of Indebtedness If Pledged	Date Pledged
a. Raw material	$	$	$	$	
b. Work in progress					
c. Finished goods					
d. Supplies					
e. Other (Specify)					
f. Total ▶	$	$	$	$	

13. Real estate

Description	Cost*	Fair Market Value	Balance Due on Mortgage	Date Mortgage Recorded	Unpaid Interest and Taxes
a.	$	$	$		$
b.					
c.					
d.					
e.					
f.					
g.					
h.					
i. Total ▶	$	$	$		$

14. Furniture and fixtures — Machinery and equipment

Description	Cost*	Liquidation Value	Amount of Indebtedness If Pledged	Date Pledged
a. Furniture and fixtures (Business)	$	$	$	
b. Furniture (Household-residence)				
c. Machinery (Specify kind)				
d.				
e.				
f.				
g. Equipment (Except trucks and automobiles) (Specify)				
h.				
i.				
j.				
k. Total ▶	$	$	$	

15. Trucks and automobiles

	Cost*	Liquidation Value	Amount of Indebtedness If Pledged	Date Pledged
a. Trucks	$	$	$	
b.				
c.				
d.				
e.				
f.				
g. Automobiles (Personal or used in business)				
h.				
i.				
j.				
k.				
l.				
m. Total ▶	$	$	$	

(*Less depreciation, if any)
Form **433** (Rev. 2-82)

Figure 4.1 Statement of Financial Condition and Other Information (Continued)

16.	Securities (Bonds, stocks, etc.)					
Name of company	Number of Units	Cost	Fair Market Value	Amount of Indebtedness If Pledged	Date Pledged
a.		$	$	$	
b.					
c.					
d.					
e.					
f.					
g.					
h.					
i. Total ▶		S	S	S	

17.	Judgments			
Name of Creditor	Amount of Judgment	Date Recorded	Where Recorded
a.	$		
b.			
c.			
d.			
e. Total ▶	S		

18. Statement of income — Corporation

IMPORTANT: If the offer in compromise is from a corporation, please furnish the information requested below *(from income tax returns, as adjusted, for past 2 years and from records for current year from January 1 to date).*

	19	19	Jan. 1 to 19
a. **Gross income**			
(1) Gross sales or receipts *(Subtract returns and allowances)*	$	$	S
(2) Cost of goods sold			
(3) Gross profit - trading or manufacturing			
(4) Gross profit - from other sources			
(5) Interest income			
(6) Rents and royalties			
(7) Gains and losses *(From Schedule D)*			
(8) Dividends			
(9) Other *(Specify)*			
(10) **Total income** ▶	$	$	$
b. **Deductions**			
(1) Compensation of officers	S	$	$
(2) Salaries and wages *(Not deducted elsewhere)*			
(3) Rents			
(4) Repairs			
(5) Bad Debts			
(6) Interest			
(7) Taxes			
(8) Losses			
(9) Dividends			
(10) Depreciation and depletion			
(11) Contributions			
(12) Advertising			
(13) Other *(Specify)*			
(14)			
(15) **Total deductions** ▶	$	$	$
c. **Net income** *(loss)* ▶	$	$	$
d. **Nontaxable income** ▶	$	$	$
e. **Unallowable deductions** ▶	$	$	$

Page 5   Form **433** (Rev. 2-82)

Figure 4.1 Statement of Financial Condition and Other Information (Continued)

19.   Salaries paid to principal officers and dividends distributed — Corporation

IMPORTANT: If the offer in compromise is from a corporation, please show salaries paid to principal officers for past 3 years and amounts distributed in dividends, if any, during and since the taxable years covered by this offer.

a. Salaries paid to (Name and Title)

	19	19	19
(1) , President	$	$	$
(2) , Vice President			
(3) , Treasurer			
(4) , Secretary			
(5)			
(6)			
(7) Total ▶	$	$	$

b.

Year	Dividends Paid		Year	Dividends Paid		Year	Dividends Paid
(1)	$	(8)		$	(15)		$
(2)		(9)			(16)		
(3)		(10)			(17)		
(4)		(11)			(18)		
(5)		(12)			(19)		
(6)		(13)					
(7)	$	(14)		$	(20) Total		$

20.   Statement of income — Individual

IMPORTANT: If the offer in compromise is from an individual or an estate, please furnish information requested below *(from income tax returns as adjusted for past 2 years).*

a. Gross income

		19	19
(1)	Salaries, wages, commissions	$	$
(2)	Dividends		
(3)	Interest		
(4)	Income from business or profession		
(5)	Partnership income		
(6)	Gains or losses *(From Schedule D, Form 1040)*		
(7)	Annuities and pensions		
(8)	Rents and royalties		
(9)	Income from estates and trusts		
(10)			
(11)			
(12)			
(13)			
(14)			
(15)	**Total income** ▶	$	$

b. Deductions

(1)	Contributions	$	$
(2)	Interest paid		
(3)	Taxes paid		
(4)	Casualty losses *(by fire, storm, etc.)*		
(5)	Medical expenses		
(6)	Bad debts		
(7)			
(8)			
(9)			
(10)			
(11)			
(12)	**Total deductions** ▶	$	$
c.	**Net income (loss)** ▶	$	$
d.	**Nontaxable income** ▶	$	$
e.	**Unallowable deductions** ▶	$	$

Form 433 (Rev. 2-82)

Figure 4.1 Statement of Financial Condition and Other Information (Continued)

21. Receipts and disbursements — Individual	From	To

If the offer in compromise is from an individual or on behalf of an estate, please furnish below a complete analysis of receipts and disbursements for the past 12 months.

a. Receipts

	Description	Source From Which Received	Amount
(1)	Salary		$
(2)	Commissions		
(3)	Business or profession		
(4)	Dividends		
(5)	Interest		
(6)	Annuities or pensions		
(7)	Rents and royalties		
(8)	Sale of assets (Net amount received)		
(9)	Amounts borrowed		
(10)	Gifts		
(11)			
(12)			
(13)			
(14)			
(15)			
(16)			
(17)			
(18)			
	Total receipts ▶		$

b. Disbursements

	Description	Amount
(1)	Debt reduction	$
(2)	Interest	
(3)	Federal taxes	
(4)	Other taxes	
(5)	Insurance premiums	
(6)	Medical expenses	
(7)	Automobile expenses	
(8)	Servant's wages	
(9)	Gifts	
(10)	Living expenses (Itemize)	
	Total disbursements ▶	$

Form **433** (Rev. 2-82)

Figure 4.1 Statement of Financial Condition and Other Information (Continued)

22. Disposal of assets—From the beginning of the taxable period covered by this offer in compromise to the present date, have you disposed of any assets or property with a cost or fair market value of more than $500, except for full value at the time of sale, transfer, exchange, gift or other disposition?

☐ No   ☐ Yes *(If yes, please furnish the following information)*

Description of Asset	Date of Transfer	Fair Market Value When Transferred	Consideration Received	Relationship of Transferee to Taxpayer
		$	$	

23. Interest in or beneficiary of estate or trust — Have you any life interest or remainder interest, either vested or contingent in any trust or estate, or are you a beneficiary of any trust?

☐ No   ☐ Yes *(If yes, please furnish a copy of the instrument creating the trust or estate — Also give the following information)*

Name of Trust or Estate	Present Value of Assets	Value of Your Interest	Annual Income Received From This Source
	$	$	$

24. Grantor, donor, trustee or fiduciary — Are you the grantor or donor of any trust, or the trustee or fiduciary for any trust?

☐ No   ☐ Yes *(If yes, please furnish a copy of the instrument creating the trust. Also give present value of corpus of trust, and any other pertinent information.)*

25. Any other assets or interests in assets — Have you any other assets or an interest in assets either actual or contingent, other than those listed here (i.e., Profit-sharing plan or pension plan)?

☐ No   ☐ Yes *(If yes, please describe the assets)*

26a. Are foreclosure proceedings pending on any real estate which you own or have an interest in? ☐ No ☐ Yes	**b.** If yes, please give location of real estate.	**c.** Was the government made a party to the suit? ☐ No ☐ Yes

27a. Are bankruptcy or receivership proceedings pending? ☐ No ☐ Yes	**b.** If a corporation, is it in process of liquidation? ☐ No ☐ Yes

28. Is the sum offered in compromise borrowed money? *(If yes, please give name and address of lender and list collateral, if any, pledged to secure the loan.)*

☐ No   ☐ Yes

29. What is the prospect of an increase in value of assets or in present income? *(Please give general statement)*

30.   **Affidavit**

Under penalties of perjury, I declare that I have examined the information given in this statement and, to the best of my knowledge and belief, it is true, correct, and complete, and I further declare that I have no assets, owned either directly or indirectly, or income of any nature other than as shown in this statement.

a. Date of this statement	b. Signature

         Form **433** (Rev. 2-82)

Figure 4.2 Collection Information Statement for Individuals

Form **433-A** (Rev. October 1992)	Department of the Treasury — Internal Revenue Service **Collection Information Statement for Individuals**

NOTE: Complete all blocks, except shaded areas. Write "N/A" *(not applicable)* **in those blocks that do not apply.**

1. Taxpayer(s) name(s) and address	2. Home phone number ( )	3. Marital status
County _____	4.a. Taxpayer's social security number	b. Spouse's social security number

Section I.   Employment Information

5. Taxpayer's employer or business *(name and address)*	a. How long employed	b. Business phone number ( )	c. Occupation
	d. Number of exemptions claimed on Form W-4	e. Paydays	f. *(Check appropriate box)* ☐ Wage earner ☐ Partner ☐ Sole proprietor

6. Spouse's employer or business *(name and address)*	a. How long employed	b. Business phone number ( )	c. Occupation
	d. Number of exemptions claimed on Form W-4	e. Paydays	f. *(Check appropriate box)* ☐ Wage earner ☐ Partner ☐ Sole proprietor

Section II.   Personal Information

7. Name, address and telephone number of next of kin or other reference	8. Other names or aliases	9. Previous address(es)

10. Age and relationship of dependents living in your household *(exclude yourself and spouse)*

11. Date of Birth ▶	a. Taxpayer	b. Spouse	12. Latest filed income tax return *(tax year)*	a. Number of exemptions claimed	b. Adjusted Gross Income

Section III.   General Financial Information

13. Bank accounts *(Include Savings & Loans, Credit Unions, IRA and Retirement Plans, Certificates of Deposit, etc.)*

Name of Institution	Address	Type of Account	Account No.	Balance
			Total *(Enter in Item 21)*	

Form **433-A** (Rev. 10-92)

Figure 4.2 Collection Information Statement for Individuals (Continued)

Section III - *continued*   General Financial Information

14. Bank charge cards, Credit Unions, Savings and Loans, Lines of credit

Type of Account or Card	Name and Address of Financial Institution	Monthly Payment	Credit Limit	Amount Owed	Credit Available
Totals *(Enter in Item 27)* ▶					

15. Safe deposit boxes rented or accessed *(List all locations, box numbers, and contents.)*

16.	Real Property *(Brief description and type of ownership)*	Physical Address
a.		
		County _____
b.		
		County _____
c.		
		County _____

17.	Life Insurance *(Name of Company)*	Policy Number	Type	Face Amount	Available Loan Value
		Total *(Enter in Item 23)* ▶			

18. Securities *(stocks, bonds, mutual funds, money market funds, government securities, etc.)*:

Kind	Quantity or Denomination	Current Value	Where Located	Owner of Record

19. Other information relating to your financial condition. If you check the yes box, please give dates and explain on page 4, Additional Information or Comments:

a. Court proceedings	☐ Yes ☐ No	b. Bankruptcies	☐ Yes ☐ No
c. Repossessions	☐ Yes ☐ No	d. Recent transfer of assets for less than full value	☐ Yes ☐ No
e. Anticipated increase in income	☐ Yes ☐ No	f. Participant or beneficiary to trust, estate, profit sharing, etc.	☐ Yes ☐ No

Form **433-A**   page 2   (Rev. 10-92)

Figure 4.2 Collection Information Statement for Individuals (Continued)

Section IV.		Asset and Liability Analysis						
Description		Current Market Value	Liabilities Balance Due	Equity in Asset	Amount of Monthly Payment	Name and Address of Lien/Note Holder/Obligee	Date Pledged	Date of Final Payment
20. Cash								
21. Bank accounts *(from Item 13)*								
22. Securities *(from Item 18)*								
23. Cash or loan value of Insur.								
24. Vehicles *(Model, year, license, tag#)*								
	a.							
	b.							
	c.							
25. Real property *(From Section III, Item 16)*	a.							
	b.							
	c.							
26. Other assets								
	a.							
	b.							
	c.							
	d.							
	e.							
27. Bank revolving credit *(from Item 14)*								
28. Other Liabilities *(Including judgments, notes, and other charge accounts)*	a.							
	b.							
	c.							
	d.							
	e.							
	f.							
	g.							
29. Federal taxes owed								
30. Totals				$	$			

Internal Revenue Service Use Only Below This Line

Financial Verification/Analysis

Item	Date Information or Encumbrance Verified	Date Property Inspected	Estimated Forced Sale Equity
Personal Residence			
Other Real Property			
Vehicles			
Other Personal Property			
State Employment *(Husband and Wife)*			
Income Tax Return			
Wage Statements *(Husband and Wife)*			
Sources of Income/Credit *(D&B Report)*			
Expenses			
Other Assets/Liabilities			

Form **433-A**   page 3   (Rev. 10-92)

Figure 4.2 Collection Information Statement for Individuals (Continued)

Section V. Monthly Income and Expense Analysis

Income			Necessary Living Expenses	
Source	**Gross**	**Net**		
31. Wages/Salaries *(Taxpayer)*	$	$	42. Rent *(Do not show mortgage listed in item 25)*	$
32. Wages/Salaries *(Spouse)*			43. Groceries (no. of people _____)	
33. Interest - Dividends			44. Allowable installment payments *(IRS use only)*	
34. Net business income *(from Form 433-B)*			45. Utilities (Gas $_____ Water $_____	
35. Rental Income			Electric $_____ Phone $_____)	
36. Pension *(Taxpayer)*			46. Transportation	
37. Pension *(Spouse)*			47. Insurance (Life $_____ Health $_____	
38. Child Support			Home $_____ Car $_____)	
39. Alimony			48. Medical *(Expenses not covered in item 47)*	
40. Other			49. Estimated tax payments	
			50. Court ordered payments	
			51. Other expenses *(specify)*	
41. Total Income	$	$	52. **Total Expenses** *(IRS use only)*	$
			53. Net difference *(income less (IRS necessary living expenses) use only)*	$

Certification Under penalties of perjury, I declare that to the best of my knowledge and belief this statement of assets, liabilities, and other information is true, correct, and complete.

54. Your signature	55. Spouse's signature *(if joint return was filed)*	56. Date

Additional information or comments:

Internal Revenue Service Use Only Below This Line

Explain any difference between Item 53 and the installment agreement payment amount:

Name of originator and IDRS assignment number:	Date

Form **433-A**   page 4   (Rev. 10-92)

★U.S.GPO:1992-0-343-049/71911

Figure 4.3 Collection Information Statement for Businesses

Form **433-B**
(Rev. June 1991)

Department of the Treasury — Internal Revenue Service

Collection Information Statement for Businesses
(If you need additional space, please attach a separate sheet)

NOTE: Complete all blocks, except shaded areas. Write "N/A" *(not applicable)* **in those blocks that do not apply.**

1. Name and address of business	2. Business phone number ( )
	3. *(Check appropriate box)* ☐ Sole proprietor ☐ Partnership ☐ Corporation ☐ Other *(specify)*
County_____	

4. Name and title of person being interviewed	5. Employer Identification Number	6. Type of business

7. Information about owner, partners, officers, major shareholder, etc.

Name and Title	Effective Date	Home Address	Phone Number	Social Security Number	Total Shares or Interest

Section I.   General Financial Information

8. Latest filed income tax return ▶	Form	Tax Year ended	Net income before taxes

9. Bank accounts *(List all types of accounts including payroll and general, savings, certificates of deposit, etc.)*

Name of Institution	Address	Type of Account	Account Number	Balance
		Total *(Enter in Item 17)* ▶		

10. Bank credit available *(Lines of credit, etc.)*

Name of Institution	Address	Credit Limit	Amount Owed	Credit Available	Monthly Payments
Totals *(Enter in Items 24 or 25 as appropriate)* ▶					

11. Location, box number, and contents of all safe deposit boxes rented or accessed

Figure 4.3 Collection Information Statement for Businesses (Continued)

Section I - *continued*   General Financial Information

12. Real property

Brief Description and Type of Ownership	Physical Address
a.	
	County _____
b.	
	County _____
c.	
	County _____
d.	
	County _____

13. Life insurance policies owned with business as beneficiary

Name Insured	Company	Policy Number	Type	Face Amount	Available Loan Value
	Total *(Enter in Item 19)*		▶		

14a. Additional information regarding financial condition *(Court proceedings, bankruptcies filed or anticipated, transfers of assets for less than full value, changes in market conditions, etc.; include information regarding company participation in trusts, estates, profit-sharing plans, etc.)*

b. If you know of any person or organization that borrowed or otherwise provided funds to pay net payrolls:	a. Who borrowed funds?
	b. Who supplied funds?

15. Accounts/Notes receivable *(Include current contract jobs, loans to stockholders, officers, partners, etc.)*

Name	Address	Amount Due	Date Due	Status
		$		
	Total *(Enter in Item 18)* ▶	$		

Form **433-B** (Rev. 6-91)

Figure 4.3 Collection Information Statement for Businesses
(Continued)

Section II.		Asset and Liability Analysis						
Description (a)		Cur. Mkt. Value (b)	Liabilities Bal. Due (c)	Equity in Asset (d)	Amt. of Mo. Pymt. (e)	Name and Address of Lien/Note Holder/Obligee (f)	Date Pledged (g)	Date of Final Pymt. (h)
16. Cash on hand								
17. Bank accounts								
18. Accounts/Notes receivable								
19. Life insurance loan value								
20. Real property *(from Item 12)*	a.							
	b.							
	c.							
	d.							
21. Vehicles *(Model, year, and license)*	a.							
	b.							
	c.							
22. Machinery and equipment *(Specify)*	a.							
	b.							
	c.							
23. Merchandise inventory *(Specify)*	a.							
	b.							
24. Other assets *(Specify)*	a.							
	b.							
25. Other liabilities *(Including notes and judgments)*	a.							
	b.							
	c.							
	d.							
	e.							
	f.							
	g.							
	h.							
26. Federal taxes owed								
27. **Total**								

Form 433-B (Rev. 6-91)

Figure 4.3   Collection Information Statement for Businesses (Continued)

Section III.   Income and Expense Analysis

The following information applies to income and expenses during the period _____ to _____	Accounting method used

Income		Expenses	
28. Gross receipts from sales, services, etc.	$	34. Materials purchased	$
29. Gross rental income		35. Net wages and salaries Number of Employees _____	
30. Interest		36. Rent	
31. Dividends		37. Allowable installment payments *(IRS use only)*	
32. Other income *(Specify)*		38. Supplies	
		39. Utilities/Telephone	
		40. Gasoline/Oil	
		41. Repairs and maintenance	
		42. Insurance	
		43. Current taxes	
		44. Other *(Specify)*	
33. Total Income ▶	$	45. Total Expenses *(IRS use only)* ▶	$
		46. Net difference *(IRS use only)* ▶	$

Certification   Under penalties of perjury, I declare that to the best of my knowledge and belief this statement of assets, liabilities, and other information is true, correct, and complete.

47. Signature	48. Date

Internal Revenue Service Use Only Below This Line

Financial Verification/Analysis

Item	Date Information or Encumbrance Verified	Date Property Inspected	Estimated Forced Sale Equity
Sources of Income/Credit (D&B Report)			
Expenses			
Real Property			
Vehicles			
Machinery and Equipment			
Merchandise			
Accounts/Notes Receivable			
Corporate Information, if Applicable			
U.C.C. : Senior/Junior Lienholder			
Other Assets/Liabilities:			

Explain any difference between Item 46 (or P&L) and the installment agreement payment amount:

Name of Originator and IDRS assignment number	Date

Figure 4.4 Installment Agreement

| Form **433-D** (Rev. January 1993) | Department of the Treasury — Internal Revenue Service **Installment Agreement** |

Name and address of taxpayer(s)	Social security or employer identification number
SAMPLE **This form is completed by the IRS and sent to the taxpayer after an agreement has been negotiated.**	*(primary)* *(secondary)*
	Kinds of taxes *(Form numbers)*
	Tax periods
	Amount owed as of _____ Earliest CSED $

Telephone: *(Home)* *(Business)*	Employer *(Name and address)*	Banks *(Names and addresses)*

I/We agree that the Federal taxes shown above, PLUS ALL PENALTIES AND INTEREST PROVIDED BY LAW, will be paid as follows:

$ _____ will be paid on _____ and $ _____ will be paid

no later than the _____ of each month thereafter until the total liability is paid in full. I/we also agree that the above

installment payment will be increased or decreased as follows:

Date of increase *(or decrease)*	/ /	/ /	For assistance:
Amount of increase *(or decrease)*	$		Call: 1-800-829-1040 or write: _____ Service Ctr.
New installment amount	$		City, State, Zip Code

Conditions of this agreement:

- Each payment must be received by the date shown above; if you have a problem, contact us immediately.
- This agreement is based on your current financial circumstances; it is subject to revision or termination if subsequent financial information required by IRS reflects a change in your ability to pay.
- Failure to provide updated financial information when requested by the Service will be reason for termination of this agreement.
- All Federal tax returns and Federal taxes that become due while this agreement is in effect must be filed and paid on time.
- Any Federal or State refunds that you are entitled to will be applied to this liability until it is satisfied. (For Alaska residents, this includes the Alaska Permanent Fund dividend.)

Additional Conditions:

- If the Conditions of this agreement are not met, it will be terminated and the entire tax liability may be collected by levy on income, bank accounts, or any other assets, or by seizure of your property.
- This agreement may be terminated if collection of the tax is in jeopardy.
- All payments will be applied in the best interest of the United States.
- This agreement is subject to acceptance by the Collection Division and may require managerial approval; if it is not accepted or approved, you will be notified.

- A NOTICE OF FEDERAL TAX LIEN *(check one)*
  - ☐ HAS ALREADY BEEN FILED
  - ☐ WILL BE FILED IMMEDIATELY
  - ☐ WILL BE FILED WHEN TAX IS ASSESSED
  - ☐ MAY BE FILED IF THIS AGREEMENT DEFAULTS

Your signature	Title *(if corporate officer or partner)*	Date	Originator's name, title and IDRS assignment number *(or district):*
Spouse's signature *(if joint liability)*		Date	
Agreement examined or approved by *(signature, title, function)*		Date	Originator Code:

YOU MAY HAVE YOUR INSTALLMENT AGREEMENT PAYMENT DEDUCTED FROM YOUR CHECKING ACCOUNT EACH MONTH (DIRECT DEBIT); IF YOU CHOOSE THIS OPTION, FOLLOW THE DIRECTIONS ON THE REVERSE SIDE OF YOUR COPY OF THIS FORM.

If you agree to Direct Debit, initial here:

- I (we) authorize the IRS and the Depository (bank) identified on the attached voided check to deduct payments (debit) from my (our) checking account or correct errors on the account. This authorization remains in effect until I (or either of us) notify IRS in writing to stop or until the liability covered by this agreement is satisfied.
- I (we) understand that if the DEPOSITORY is unable to honor IRS's request for payment due to insufficient funds in my (our) account on the payment due date I (we) will be charged a penalty of $15.00 or two percent of the payment request, whichever is greater. If the payment request is for less than $15.00, the penalty is the amount of the request.

Part 1—Taxpayer's Copy   Form **433-D** (Rev. 1-93)

77

Figure 4.4 Installment Agreement (Continued)

INSTRUCTIONS TO TAXPAYER

If not already completed by an IRS employee, in the space provided, enter:

your name and current address;

your Social Security Number and/or your Employer Identification Number (whichever applies to your tax liability);

the complete name and address of your employer(s) and your bank(s);

your home and work/business telephone number(s);

the amount you are able to pay now as a partial payment;

the amount you are able to pay each month (or the amount determined by IRS personnel; and

the date you prefer to make this payment (this must be the same day for each month, from the 1st to the 28th, and it must be received by this date; if you elect the Direct Debit option, this is the day you want your account debited).

If you choose to have your monthly payment automatically deducted from your checking account (Direct Debit), put your initials in the space provided, give the Bank Copy to your bank and attach a blank, voided check to the IRS-Input Copy of this form.

On the same day each month, your checking account will automatically be debited for the amount of your monthly payment. Be sure to update your checkbook each month. There will be no reminder notices from IRS.

When you have finished, **sign and date** the Installment Agreement and return it to either the office where you received it or mail it to your service center.

If you have any questions regarding the Direct Debit process or the completion of this form, please call the toll-free number on the front of this form.

Note: When making an installment, please be sure to:

1. Write your social security or employer identification number on each payment.

2. Make each payment in an amount at least equal to that specified in this agreement.

3. Do not double one payment and skip the next without contacting us first.

4. Enclose with each payment a copy of the reminder notice (if you received one), in the envelope provided.

5. Mail your payment on time to the proper IRS office, even if you did not receive a reminder notice. (Note: we must receive it by the due date.)

6. Contact us immediately if you cannot meet the terms of this agreement.

Figure 4.5   Collection Information Statement

Form **433-F** (Rev. May 1990)	Department of the Treasury - Internal Revenue Service **Collection Information Statement** *(If you need additional space, please attach a separate sheet with your name(s) and Social Security number(s).)*

Your name(s) and address *(Including county)*	Phone numbers *(circle best daytime number)* Home: Your work: Your spouse's work:
	Social Security numbers Yours: Your Spouse's
Your employer or business *(name and address)*	Your spouse's employer or business *(name and address)*

Real estate *(Home and other Real Estate)*

County/Description	Value	Balance Owed	Equity	Monthly Payment

Other assets *(Cars, Boats, RV's, etc.)*

County/Description	Value	Balance Owed	Equity	Monthly Payment

Bank accounts *(include Savings & Loans, Credit Unions, Certificates of Deposit, Individual Retirement Accounts, Lines of Credit, etc.)*

Name of Institution	Address	Type of account	Balance

Monthly Income

Your net pay	$
Your spouse's net pay	
Social Security or Pensions	
Profit from your business	
Other income *(source)*:	
Total income	$

Monthly Expenses

Rent	$
Groceries	
Utilities *(Electricity, Heating, Gas, Water, Phone)*	
Transportation *(gas, bus fares)*	
Medical *(doctors, & medicine not paid by insurance)*	
Insurance *(Auto, Health, Life, Homeowners/Rental)*	
Estimated Tax Payment (1040ES)	
Other *(explain)*	
Credit Cards	
Loan Payments *(not listed above)*	

Additional Information *(expected changes to income, health, etc.)*

Under penalties of perjury, I declare that to the best of my knowledge and belief this statement of assets, liabilities, and other information is true, correct, and complete.

Your signature	Spouse's signature	Date

Catalog No. 62053Y   *U.S. GPO: 1992-312-711/61572   Form **433-F** (Rev. 5-90)

79

Figure 4.6 Offer in Compromise

Form **656** (Rev. February 1992)	Department of the Treasury — Internal Revenue Service # **Offer in Compromise**	▶ **File in Triplicate** ▶ **See Instructions** Page 4

Name and Address of Taxpayers

	For Official Use Only
	Offer is *(Check applicable box)* Serial Number
	☐ Cash *(Paid in full)*
	☐ Deferred payment *(Cashier's stamp)*

Social Security Number	Employer Identification Number	

To: **Commissioner of Internal Revenue Service**

Amount Paid
$

(1) This offer is being submitted by taxpayer-proponents to compromise a tax liability, plus statutory additions resulting from the failure to pay an Internal Revenue liability described

as follows: _____

(Describe the specific tax liability, see instructions)

_____

_____

_____

_____

(2) The total sum of the offer is $ _____ . If payment in full is not submitted with this offer, describe below when the payment will be made:

_____

_____

_____

As required by section 6621 of the Internal Revenue Code, interest shall accrue on payments made from the date the offer is accepted and until the amount offered is paid in full. The interest will be compounded daily as required by Section 6622 of the Internal Revenue Code.

(3) All payments made with this offer are submitted voluntarily. The taxpayer-proponents request that the offer be accepted to compromise the tax liability described in paragraph (1). If the offer is rejected or withdrawn, the amount deposited will be refunded unless the taxpayer-proponents authorize in writing that the payment be applied to the liability. If an authorization is made, the date of payment will be considered the date the offer is rejected or withdrawn.

(4) In making this offer and as part of the consideration for the offer, the taxpayer-proponents agree: (a) to comply with all the provisions of the Internal Revenue Code relating to the filing of returns and the paying of taxes for a period of five (5) years following the acceptance of the offer; (b) that the United States shall retain all payments and credits made and applied to the tax liabilities being compromised, until the terms of the offer are satisfied; (c) that the United States shall be entitled to keep all amounts, including interest and penalties due to the taxpayer-proponents under the Internal Revenue laws because of any overpayment of any tax or other liability, for periods ending before the calendar year or extending through the calendar year in which the offer is accepted, and (d) to immediately return to the Internal Revenue Service any overpayment amount identified in (c) above, following the acceptance of the offer.

(5) The total amount that can be collected under the terms and conditions of this offer cannot exceed the amount of the tax liabilities being compromised plus statutory additions.

(6) It is also agreed that payments made under the terms of the offer shall be applied first to tax and penalty, in that order, due for the earliest tax period covered by this offer, then to tax and penalty for each succeeding tax period covered by this offer. No amount shall be applied to payment of interest until the tax and penalty liabilities for all tax periods covered by this offer have been paid.

(7) It is agreed that upon notice to the taxpayer-proponents that the offer has been accepted, the taxpayer-proponents shall have no right to contest in court or otherwise the amount of the liability to be compromised. In addition, if there is a default on any payment or any other condition required under the terms of the offer, the Commissioner of the Internal Revenue Service or delegated official, may (a) proceed immediately by suit to collect the entire unpaid balance of the offer; (b) proceed immediately by suit to collect as liquidated damages an amount equal to the liability sought to be compromised, minus any payments already received under the terms of the offer with interest on the unpaid balance accruing and applied as specified in paragraph (2), from the date of default; or (c) disregard the amount of the offer and apply all amounts previously paid under the offer against the amount of the liability compromised and, without further notice of any kind, assess and collect by levy or suit the balance of the liability. The right to appeal to the United States Tax Court and the statutory restrictions against assessment and collection are waived upon acceptance of this offer as stated in paragraph (8).

(8) The taxpayer-proponents agree to the waiver and suspension of any statutory periods of limitations for assessment and collection of the tax liability described in paragraph (1) while the offer is pending, during the time any amount offered remains unpaid and for one (1) year after the satisfaction of the terms of the offer. The offer shall be deemed pending from the date an authorized official of the Internal Revenue Service accepts taxpayer-proponents' waiver of the statutory periods of limitation and shall remain pending until an authorized official of the Internal Revenue Service formally, in writing, accepts, rejects or withdraws the offer. If there is an appeal with respect to this offer, the offer shall be deemed pending until the date the Appeals office formally accepts or rejects this offer in writing. If within thirty (30) days of being notified of a right to protest a determination with regard to this offer, no protest is filed, the taxpayer-proponents agree to waive the right to a hearing before the Appeals office for this offer in compromise.

(9) The following facts and reasons are submitted as grounds for acceptance of this offer: _____

_____

_____

(If space is insufficient, please attach a supporting statement)

(10) It is understood that this offer will be considered and acted upon in due course and that it does not relieve the taxpayers from the liability sought to be compromised unless and until the offer is accepted in writing by the Commissioner or a delegated official, and there has been full compliance with the terms of the offer.

I accept the waiver of statutory period of limitations for the Internal Revenue Service.	Under penalties of perjury, I declare that I have examined this offer, including accompanying schedules and statements, and to the best of my knowledge and belief, it is true, correct and complete.	
Signature of authorized Internal Revenue Service Official	Signature of Taxpayer-proponent	Date
Title Date	Signature of Taxpayer-proponent	Date

Part 1 IRS Copy   Form **656** (Rev. 2-92)

Figure 4.6 Offer in Compromise (Continued)

For Office Use Only		
Liability Incurred By *(List taxpayers included under same account no.)*	Kind of Liability *(Complete description)*	
Date Notice of Lien Filed	Place Notice of Lien Filed	Was Bond Filed? *(If yes, attach copy)* ☐ Yes ☐ No
Were Assets Pledged as Security? *(If yes, attach complete information)*	Periods Involved and Dates Returns Filed for Offers Involving Delinquency Penalties Only	Were Tax Collection Waivers Filed? *(If yes, attach copies)* ☐ Yes ☐ No
Attach Transcript of Accounts		

Part 2 IRS Copy   Form **656** (Rev. 2-92)

Figure 4.6 Offer in Compromise (Continued)

Page 4

Instructions

Background

Section 7122 of the Internal Revenue Code allows delegated Service officials to compromise a tax liability prior to its being referred to the Department of Justice. The term "tax liability" includes all penalty, interest, additional amount or addition to tax.

Reason for Compromise

The service is allowed to compromise a liability for only one (1) or both of the following two (2) reasons:

(1) doubt as to whether the taxpayer owes the liability
(2) doubt that the liability can be collected in full

The Service cannot legally accept a compromise where the liability has already been decided by a court and/or there is no doubt that the liability can be collected.

If If you are submitting an offer based on doubt that the liability is owed, you must include with Form 656 a written statement which describes in detail why you believe that you do not owe the liability. If you are making the offer based on doubt as to our ability to collect your liability, you must include with Form 656 a statement which describes in detail why you believe the Service cannot collect more than offered from your assets and your present and future income, taking into consideration that the Service generally has ten (10) years to collect your liability. If you have assets or income which may be available to you but not to the Service for collection action, you must also explain why we should not expect some portion of these assets or income to be paid to the Service if we are to compromise your liability for less than you owe.

Service Policy

The Service will accept an offer in compromise when it is unlikely that the tax liability can be collected in full and the amount offered reasonably reflects collection potential. An offer in compromise is a legitimate alternative to declaring a case as currently not collectible or to a protracted installment agreement. The goal is to achieve collection of what is potentially collectible at the earliest possible time and at the least cost to the Government.

In cases where an offer in compromise appears to be a viable solution to a tax delinquency, the Service employee assigned the case will discuss the compromise alternative with the taxpayer and, when necessary, assist in preparing the required forms. The taxpayer will be responsible for initiating the first specific proposal for compromise.

The success of the compromise program will be assured only if taxpayers make adequate compromise proposal consistent with their ability to pay and the Service makes prompt and reasonable decisions. Taxpayers are expected to provide reasonable documentation to verify their ability to pay. The ultimate goal is a compromise which is in the best interest of both the taxpayer and the Service. Acceptance of an adequate offer will also result in creating for the taxpayer an expectation of and a fresh start towards compliance with all future filing and payment requirements.

Practical Consideration

The Service's policy is that the ultimate goal is a settlement which is both in the best interests of the Government and the taxpayer. It is your responsibility to show us why it would be in the Government's best interest to accept your proposal. When we consider your offer we must ask ourselves the following questions:

(1) Could we collect more from the taxpayer than is offered? If the answer is "yes", you will either have to submit a larger offer or we must reject your offer.

(2) Would we be better off waiting until some date in the future because all the evidence would indicate that collection in the future would result in more money than is offered? If the answer is "yes", you will either have to submit a larger offer amount or we must reject your offer.

(3) Would the taxpaying public believe that the acceptance of your offer was a correct action. If the answer is "no", you either have to submit a larger offer or we would have to reject your offer.

The fact that you have no assets or income at this time from which the Service could collect the liability does not mean that the Service should simply accept anything that is offered because it represents all we can collect now. The Service does not operate on the theory that "something is better than nothing". For example it would not generally be in the Service's best interests to accept $25 on a $1,000 dollars liability or $1,000 on a $100,000 liability. It would generally be better for the Service to reject such nominal amount and wait to see what collection potential would arise during the remaining period of our ten-year collection period.

As we state in our policy, your offer will only be successful if, you submit a legitimate proposal that is in the Government's best interests.

Additional Consideration

Generally the Service believes that you benefit if we accept your offer because you can conduct your financial life without the burden of a tax liability. Therefore, we may require further consideration for acceptance of your offer through the use of the following:

(1) A written agreement that will require you to pay a percentage of future earnings.

(2) A written agreement to relinquish certain present or potential tax benefits.

Tax Compliance

Generally the Service will not accept an offer unless it is clear that the taxpayer will comply with all current filing requirements. You will note that the terms of the offer require future compliance for a period of five (5) years. Additionally, we will not accept your offer if you are not complying with all your current filing and paying requirements.

Withholding Collection

Submission of an offer does not automatically suspend collection action on a liability. If there is any indication that the filing of the offer is solely for the purpose of delaying the collection of the tax or that delay would negatively impact our ability to collect the tax, we will continue collection efforts. If you have reached an agreement with the Service to make installment payments, those payments should continue.

Specific Instructions

(1) Form 656, Offer in Compromise, must be used to submit an offer. The form is prepared in triplicate and filed in the district office of the Internal Revenue Service in your area. if you have been working with a specific service employee on your case, file the offer with that employee.

(2) Form 433-A, Collection Information Statement for individuals and/or Form 433-B Collection Information Statement for Business, must accompany Form 656, if the offer is being submitted on the basis of doubt as to collectibility. In order for the offer to be considered, all blocks on forms 433-A and 433-B must be completed. In those blocks that do affect you indicate by writing "N/A" (not applicable). When you submit Form 433-A and/or 433-B documentation should be submitted to verify values of assets, encumbrances and income and expense information listed on the collection information statement.

(3) Your full name, address and taxpayer identification number must be entered at the top of Form 656. If this is a joint liability (husband and wife) and both wish to make an offer, both names must be shown. If you are singly liable for a liability (e.g. employment taxes) and at the same time jointly liable for another liability (e.g. income taxes) and only one person is submitting an offer, only one offer must be submitted. If you are singly liable for one liability and jointly liable for another and both joint parties are submitting an offer, two (2) Forms 656 must be submitted, one (1) for the separate liability and one (1) for the joint liability.

(4) You must list all unpaid liabilities to be compromised in item (1) on Form 656. The type of tax and the period of the liability must be specifically identified. Examples of the most common liabilities and the proper identification you should use are as follows:

Liability	proper description
1040	Income tax for the year(s) 19XX . . .
941	Withholding and Federal Insurance Contribution Act taxes for the period(s) ended 09/30/XX, 12/31/XX . . .
940	Federal Unemployment Tax Act taxes for the year(s) 19XX . . .
100 percent penalty	100% penalty assessment incurred as a responsible person of Y Corporation for failure to pay withholding and Federal Insurance Contributions Act taxes for the periods ended 09/30/XX, 12/31/XX . . .
Failure to file penalty	Penalty for failure to file income tax return(s) for the tax year(s) 19XX . . . (Note: This is necessary only if your offer is submitted to compromise the penalty because of doubt as to liability)

(5) The total amount you are offering to compromise the liability must be entered in item (2). The amount must not include any amount which has already been paid or collected on the liability. Generally the starting place for the amount you offer should be the amount shown in item 27 column (d) in Form 433-B or line 37 titled "Equity in Assets" on form 433-A.

If any amount is to be paid on notice of acceptance of the offer or at any later date, you must include in item (2) as follows:

(a) The amount, if any, deposited at the time of filing this offer.
(b) Any amount deposited on a prior offer which are to be applied on this offer. (This does not include any amount you previously authorized the Service to apply directly to the tax liability)
(c) The amount of any subsequent payment and the date on which each payment is to be made.

Example: $30,000 – $5,000 deposited with the offer and $25,000 to be paid within ten (10) days from the date of acceptance.

Example: $103,000 – $13,000 deposited with the offer and $10,000 to be paid within ten (10) days from the date of acceptance and $10,000 paid on the 15th of each month following the month in which the offer is accepted.

The offer should be liquidated in the shortest time possible. Under no circumstances should the payment extend beyond five (5) years from the date of acceptance to the date of full payment. Interest is due at the prevailing Internal Revenue Code rate from the date of acceptance to the date of full payment.

(6) You must state in detail in item (9) why the Service should accept your offer. Attach additional pages as necessary.

(7) You must sign and date the offer in the lower right hand corner of Form 656. If you and your spouse are submitting the offer on a joint liability both must sign. If the offer is to be signed by a person other than the taxpayer, a valid power of attorney must be submitted with the offer.

What You Are Agreeing To

Please read Form 656 carefully so that you understand what you are agreeing to. Among other things you are agreeing to

1. The suspension of any statutory period for assessment and collection of the tax liability while the offer is pending, during the time any amount offered remains unpaid and for one (1) year thereafter.
2. Not to contest in court or otherwise appeal the amount of the liability if your offer is accepted.
3. The giving up of overpayments (refunds) for all tax periods prior to and including the year the offer is accepted.
4. The possible reinstatement of your entire tax liability, if you do not comply with all the terms of the offer, including the requirement for future compliance.

Public Disclosure

You should be aware that the law requires that all accepted offers in compromise be available for review by the general public. Therefore it is possible that details of your personal financial affairs may become publicly known.

*U.S. Government Printing Office: 1992 — 312-711/61531

Form 656 (Rev. 2-92)

83

Figure 4.7 IRS Tax Collection Guidelines

COLLECTION ACTIVITY

5223

Analysis of Taxpayer's Financial Condition
(1) The analysis of the taxpayer's financial condition provides the interviewer with a basis to make one or more of the following decisions:
   (a) require payment from available assets;
   (b) secure a short-term agreement or a longer installment agreement;
   (c) report the account currently not collectible;
   (d) recommend or initiate enforcement action (this would also be based on the results of the interview);
   (e) file a Notice of Federal Tax Lien; and/or
   (f) explain the offer in compromise provisions of the Code to the taxpayer.
(2) In all steps that follow, information on the financial statement will be compared with other financial information provided by the taxpayer, particularly the copy of the taxpayer's latest Form 1040. If there are significant discrepancies, they should be discussed with the taxpayer. In the event further documentation is needed, it will be the taxpayer's responsibility to provide it. Discrepancies and their resolution will be noted in the case file history.
(3) Analyze assets to determine ways of liquidating the account:
   (a) if the taxpayer has cash equal to the tax liability, demand immediate payment;
   (b) otherwise, review other assets which may be pledged or readily converted to cash (such as stocks and bonds, loan value of life insurance policies, etc.);
   (c) if necessary, review any unencumbered assets, equity in encumbered assets, interests in estates and trusts, lines of credit (including available credit on bank charge cards), etc., from which money may be secured to make payment. In addition, consider the taxpayer's ability to make an unsecured loan. If the taxpayer belongs to a credit union, the taxpayer will be asked to borrow from that source. Upon identification of potential sources of loans, establish a date that the taxpayer is expected to make payments; and
   (d) if there appears to be no borrowing ability, attempt to get the taxpayer to defer payment of other debts in order to pay the tax first.
(4) When analysis of the taxpayer's assets has given no obvious solution for liquidating the liability, the income and expenses should be analyzed.
   (a) When deciding what is an allowable expense item, the employee may allow:
      1. expenses which are necessary for the taxpayer's production of income (for example, dues for a trade union or professional organization; child care payments which allow a taxpayer to work);
      2. expenses which provide for the health and welfare of the taxpayer and family. The expense must be reasonable for the size of the

Figure 4.7   IRS Tax Collection Guidelines (Continued)

family and the geographic location, as well as any unique individual circumstances. An expense will not be allowed if it serves to provide an elevated standard of living, as opposed to basic necessities. Also, an expense will not be allowed if the taxpayer has a proven record of not making the payment. Expenses allowable under this category are:

a. rent or mortgage for place of residence;
b. food;
c. clothing;
d. necessary transportation expense (auto insurance, car payment, bus fare, etc.);
e. home maintenance expense (utilities, home-owner insurance, home-owner dues, etc.);
f. medical expenses; health insurance;
g. current tax payments (including federal, state and local);
h. life insurance, but not if it is excessive to the point of being construed as an investment;
i. alimony, child support or other court-ordered payment.

3. Minimum payments on secured or legally perfected debts (car payments, judgments, etc.) will normally be allowed. However, if the encumbered asset represents an item which would not be considered a necessary living expense (e.g., a boat, recreational vehicle, etc.), the taxpayer should be advised that the debt payment will not be included as an allowable expense.

4. Payments on unsecured debts (credit cards, personal loans, etc.) may not be allowed if omitting them would permit the taxpayer to pay in full within 90 days. However, if the taxpayer cannot fully pay within that time, minimum payments may be allowed if failure to make them would ultimately impair the taxpayer's ability to pay the tax. The taxpayer should be advised that since all necessary living expenses have been allowed, no additional charge debts should be incurred. Generally, payments to friends or relatives will not be allowed. Dates for final payments on loans or installment purchases, as well as final payments on revolving credit arrangements after allowing minimum required payments, will be noted so the additional funds will be applied to the liability when they become available. If permitting the taxpayer to pay unsecured debts results in inability to pay or in only having a small amount left for payment of the tax, the taxpayer should be advised that a portion of the money available for payment of debts will be used for payment of the taxes and that arrangements must be made with other creditors accordingly.

(b) As a general rule, expenses not specified in (a) above will be disallowed. However, an otherwise disallowable expense may be included

Figure 4.7 IRS Tax Collection Guidelines (Continued)

if the employee believes an exception should be made based on the circumstances of the individual case. For instance, if the taxpayer advises that an educational expense or church contribution is a necessity, the individual circumstances must be considered. If an exception is made, document the case history to explain the basis for the exception.

(c) The taxpayer will be required to verify and support any expense which appears excessive based on the income and circumstances of that taxpayer. However, proof of payment does not automatically make an item allowable. The criteria in (4)(a) apply.

(d) In some cases, expense items or payments will not be due in even monthly increments. For instance, personal property tax may be due once a year. Unless the taxpayer substantiates that money is being set aside on a monthly basis, the expense will be allowed in total in the month due and the payment agreement adjusted accordingly for that month. Expense items with varying monthly payments should be averaged over a twelve-month period unless the variation will be excessive. In such instances, exclude the irregular months from the average. For example, if a utility bill will be excessive during the three winter months, average the other nine months.

(e) In arriving at available net income, analyze the taxpayer's deductions to ensure that they are reasonable and allowable. The only automatically allowable deductions from gross pay or income are federal, state and local taxes (including FICA or other mandatory retirement program).

　1. Other deductions from gross pay or income will be treated and listed as expenses, but only to the extent they meet the criteria in (4)(a) above.

　2. To avoid affording the taxpayer a double deduction for one expense, ensure that such amounts remain in the total net pay figure and are also entered on the expense side of the income and expense analysis.

　3. If the exemptions on the W-4 are going to be decreased, make the appropriate adjustments in the net income figures.

(f) To reach an average monthly take-home pay for taxpayers paid on a weekly basis, multiply the weekly pay times 52 weeks divided by 12 months (or multiply amount times 4.3 weeks). If the taxpayer is paid biweekly, multiply pay times 26 weeks divided by 12 months (or multiply amount times $2 \frac{1}{6}$). If the taxpayer is paid semimonthly, multiply pay times 2.

(g) The amount to be paid monthly on an installment agreement payment will be at least the difference between the taxpayer's net income and allowable expenses. If the taxpayer will not consent to the proposed installment agreement, he/she should be advised that enforced collection action may be taken. The taxpayer should also be advised that an appeal of the matter may be made to the immediate manager.

Figure 4.7 IRS Tax Collection Guidelines (Continued)

(5) When an analysis of the taxpayer's financial condition shows that liquidation of assets and payments from present and future income will not result in full payment, consider the collection potential of an offer in compromise.

5225

Verification of Taxpayer's Financial Condition

(1) In some cases it will be necessary or desirable to obtain additional information about the taxpayer's financial condition. The extent of the investigation will depend upon the circumstances in each case.

(2) If items appear to be over- or understated, or out of the ordinary, the taxpayer should be asked to explain and substantiate if necessary. The explanation will be documented in the case history. If the explanation is unsatisfactory or cannot be substantiated, the amount should be revised appropriate to the documentation available.

5231.1

General Installment Agreement Guidelines

(1) When taxpayers state inability to pay the full amount of their taxes, installment agreements are to be considered.

(2) Future compliance with the tax laws will be addressed and any returns and/or tax due within the period of the agreement must be filed and paid timely.

(3) Levy source information, including complete addresses and ZIP codes, will be secured.

(4) Equal monthly installment payments should be requested. Payment amounts may be increased or decreased as necessary.

(5) Once the determination is made that the taxpayer has the capability to make a regular installment payment, that agreement will be monitored through routine provisions unless the payment amount is less than $10 (in which case the account should be reported currently not collectible). The major benefits of this approach are issuance of reminder and default notices (if the account is system-monitored) and enforcement action if the agreement is not kept.

(6) The taxpayer should be allowed to select the payment due date(s). But if there is no preference, the date when the taxpayer would generally be in the best financial position to make the payment(s) should be chosen.

(7) If the interviewer and the taxpayer cannot agree on the amount of installments, the taxpayer should be advised that an appeal may be made to the immediate manager.

(8) An installment agreement which lasts more than two years must be reviewed at the mid-point of the agreement, but in no event less than every two years.

Figure 4.8 Levy and Sale

5311

Introduction and General Concepts

(1) Under the Internal Revenue Code, levy is defined as the power to collect taxes by distraint or seizure of the taxpayer's assets. Through levy, we can attach property in the possession of third parties or the taxpayer. Generally, a notice of levy is used to attach funds due the taxpayer from third parties. Levy on property in possession of the taxpayer is accomplished by seizure and public sale of the property. There is no statutory requirement as to the sequence to be followed in levying, but it is generally less burdensome and time consuming to levy on funds in possession of third parties.

(2) Levy authority is far reaching. It permits a continuous attachment of the non-exempt portion of the wage or salary payments due the taxpayer, and the seizure and sale of all the taxpayer's assets except certain property that is specifically exempt by law. Prior to levying on any property belonging to a taxpayer, the Service must notify the taxpayer in writing of the Service's intention to levy. The statute does not require a judgment or other court order before levy action is taken. The Supreme Court decision in the matter of *G.M. Leasing Corporation v. United States,* 429 U.S. 338 (1977), held that an entry without a warrant and search of private areas of both residential and business premises for the purpose of seizing and inventorying property pursuant to Internal Revenue Code section 6331 is in violation of the Fourth Amendment. Prior to seizure of property on private premises, a consent to enter for the purpose of seizing or writ of entry from the local courts must be secured.

(3) Procedures are designed (except in jeopardy cases) to give taxpayers a reasonable chance to settle their tax liabilities voluntarily before the more drastic enforcement actions are started. At least one final notice must be issued before service of a notice of levy.

(4) Under the self-assessment system, a taxpayer is entitled to a reasonable opportunity to voluntarily comply with the revenue laws. This concept should also be followed in connection with levy action. This does not mean that there should be a reluctance to levy if the circumstances justify that action. However, before levy or seizure is taken on an account, the taxpayer must be informed, except in jeopardy situations, that levy or seizure will be the next action taken and given a reasonable opportunity to pay voluntarily. Once the taxpayer has been advised and neglects to make satisfactory arrangements, levy action should be taken expeditiously, but not less than 10 days after notice.

(5) Notification prior to levy must be given in accordance with (2) above. It should be specific that levy action will be the next action taken. In the event the service center has not sent the taxpayer the 4th notice which includes notice of intention to levy at least 10 days before the levy, the revenue officer must provide the notice to the taxpayer as indicated in (2) above.

(6) A notice of levy should be served only when there is evidence or reasonable

Figure 4.8   Levy and Sale (Continued)

expectation that the third party has property or rights to property of the taxpayer. This concept is of particular significance, since processing of notices of levy is time consuming and often becomes a sensitive matter if it appears the levy action was merely a "fishing expedition."

5312

Statutory Authority to Levy

(1) IRC 6331 provides that if any person liable to pay any tax neglects or refuses to pay the tax within 10 days after notice and demand, the tax may be collected by levy upon any property or rights to property belonging to the taxpayer or on which there is a lien.

(2) IRC 6331 also provides that if the Secretary determines that the collection of tax is in jeopardy, immediate notice and demand for payment may be made and, upon the taxpayer's failure to pay the tax, collection may be made by levy without regard to the 10-day period. However, if a sale is required, a public notice of sale may not be issued within the 10-day period unless IRC 6336 (relating to sale of perishable goods) is applicable.

(3) Under the IRC, the term "property" includes all property or rights to property, whether real or personal, tangible or intangible. The term "tax" includes any interest, additional amount, addition to tax, or assessable penalty, together with any cost that may accrue.

(4) Generally, property subject to a Federal tax lien which has been sold or otherwise transferred by the taxpayer, may be levied upon in the hands of the transferee or any subsequent transferee. However, there are exceptions for securities, motor vehicles and certain retail and casual sales.

(5) Levy may be made on any person in possession of, or obligated with respect to, property or rights to property subject to levy. These include, but are not necessarily limited to, receivables, bank accounts, evidences of debt, securities and accrued salaries, wages, commissions, and other compensation.

(6) The IRC does not require that property be seized in any particular sequence. Therefore, property may be levied upon regardless of whether it is real or personal, tangible or intangible, and regardless of which type of property is levied upon first.

(7) Whenever the proceeds from the levy on any property or rights to property are not sufficient to satisfy the tax liability, additional levies may be made upon the same property, or source of income or any other property or rights to property subject to levy, until the account is fully paid. However, further levies should be timed to avoid hardship to the taxpayer or his/her family.

5314.1

Property Exempt from Levy

(1) IRC 6334 enumerates the categories of property exempt from levy as follows:

Figure 4.8 Levy and Sale (Continued)

(a) *Wearing apparel and school books necessary for the taxpayer or for members of his family*—No specific value limitation is placed on these items since the intent is to prevent seizing the ordinary clothing of the taxpayer or members of the family. Expensive items of wearing apparel, such as furs, are luxuries and are not exempt from levy.

(b) *Fuel, provisions and personal effects*—This exemption is applicable only in the case of the head of a family and applies only to so much of the fuel, provisions, furniture, and personal effects of the household and of arms for personal use, livestock, and poultry as does not exceed $1,500 in value.

(c) *Books and tools of a trade, business or profession*—This exemption is for so many of the books and tools necessary for the trade, business, or profession of the taxpayer as do not exceed in the aggregate $1,000 in value.

(d) *Unemployment benefits*—This applies to any amount payable to an individual for unemployment (including any portion payable to dependents) under an unemployment compensation law of the United States, any state, the District of Columbia or the Commonwealth of Puerto Rico.

(e) *Undelivered mail*—Addressed mail which has not been delivered to the addressee.

(f) *Certain annuity and pension payments.*

(g) *Workmen's compensation*—Any amount payable to an individual as workmen's compensation (including any portion payable to dependents) under a workmen's compensation law of the United States, any state, the District of Columbia, or the Commonwealth of Puerto Rico.

(h) *Judgment for support of minor children*—If the taxpayer is required by judgment of a court of competent jurisdiction, entered prior to the date of levy, to contribute to the support of his/her minor children, so much of his/her salary, wages, or other income as is necessary to comply with such judgment.

(i) *Minimum Exemption from Levy on Wages, Salary and Other Income*—IRC 6334(a)(9) limits the effect of levy on wages, salary and other income, by an amount of $75 per week for the taxpayer and an additional $25 a week for the spouse and each dependent claimed by the taxpayer. Income not paid or received on a weekly basis will, for the purpose of computing exemptions, be apportioned as if received on a weekly basis.

(2) In addition, Public Law 89-538 exempts deposits to the special Treasury fund made by servicemen and servicewomen (including officers) and Public Health Service employees on permanent duty assignment outside the United States or its possessions.

(3) Except for the exemptions in (1) and (2) above, no other property or rights to property are exempt from levy. No provision of state law can exempt

Figure 4.8 Levy and Sale (Continued)

property or rights to property from levy for the collection of federal taxes. The fact that property is exempt from execution under state personal or homestead exemption laws does not exempt the property from federal levy.

(4) The revenue officer seizing property of the type described in (1)(a), (b), and (c) above should appraise and set aside to the owner the amount of property to be exempted.

538(10)

Records of Attorneys, Physicians, and Accountants

(1) Records maintained by attorneys, physicians, and accountants concerning professional services performed for clients are usually of little intrinsic value and possess minimum sale value. Questions of confidential or privileged information contained in these records may cause complications if the records are seized. Additionally, the case files of the professional person frequently either are, or contain, property of the client, and therefore to this extent are not subject to seizure. Accordingly, it is not believed desirable to seize case files or records for payment of the taxpayer's tax liabilities.

(2) When office facilities or office equipment of attorneys, physicians, or public accountants are seized for payment of taxes, case files and related files in seized office facilities or office equipment of such persons will not be personally examined by the revenue officer even though information concerning accounts receivable may be contained in the files. When storage facilities (filing cabinets, etc.) are seized, the taxpayer should be requested to remove all case files promptly.

583(11)

Safe Deposit Boxes

538(11).1

General

(1) The procedures outlined below should be followed in an attempt to secure the opening of a taxpayer's safe deposit box in instances in which the taxpayer's consent to or cooperation in opening the box cannot be obtained.

(2) Ordinarily two keys are used to open a safe deposit box: a master key held by the bank or trust company which owns the box and an individual key in the possession of the person who rents the box.

(3) Irrespective of the possession of the necessary equipment to do so, it is not to be expected that a bank or trust company will open a safe deposit box without the consent of the lessee of the box unless protected by a court order. Under these circumstances the government must prevent the taxpayer from having access to the box, or obtain a court order directing that the box be opened, by force if necessary.

Figure 4.8 Levy and Sale (Continued)

(4) At the time that a safety deposit is secured, Publication 787, Seal for Securing Safety Deposit Boxes, will be signed by the revenue officer and affixed over the locks for security while the box remains under seizure. When the box is eventually opened, all residue from the seal should be removed by the revenue officer, or the bank official in the revenue officer's presence, with isopropyl alcohol or a similar solvent. To avoid damage to the safety deposit box, no sharp implement or abrasive substance should be used. The seal will dissolve when saturated with alcohol and rubbed with a cloth.

583(11).2

Preventing Access to Safe Deposit Box

(1) A notice of lien should be filed prior to seizure since assets other than cash may be in the safe deposit box.

(2) A notice of levy, Form 668-A, with a copy of the notice of lien attached, should be served on an officer of the bank or trust company and request made for surrender of the contents of the box.

(3) The official may advise that the institution does not have the necessary key to open the safe deposit box or that the institution does not have the authority to open it. He/she may also suggest that the lessee's (taxpayer's) consent be secured, or that a court order be obtained to open the box.

(4) Under these circumstances, the revenue officer should not insist that the box be opened and no attempt should be made to have the box opened by force. The box should be sealed by affixing a seizure notice, Publication 787, Seal for Securing Safety Deposit Boxes. It should be placed over the locks in such a manner so that the box cannot be opened without removing, tearing or destroying the affixed seal. The bank or trust company should then be advised not to permit the box to be opened except in the presence of a revenue officer.

(5) Usually, taxpayers who have been reluctant to cooperate will eventually find it necessary to open their boxes, and will only be able to do so in the presence of a revenue officer. At that time, the revenue officer, with Form 668-B in his/her possession, will be in a position to seize any property in the box.

(6) When the rental period of the safe deposit box expires and is not renewed, a bank or trust company usually has the right and power to open the box. The revenue officer should attempt to ascertain the true situation in any given case, and if the right and power exists, should try to take advantage of this opportunity to seize the contents of the box.

538(11).3

Obtaining Court Order To Open

(1) Occasionally, the procedure outlined in IRM 538(11).2 will not be satisfactory and immediate action may be desirable or necessary. For instance, the

Figure 4.8   Levy and Sale (Continued)

statute of limitations may be about to expire, the taxpayer may have disappeared or be in concealment, or the taxpayer or bank officials may refuse cooperation and deny access to a safe deposit box.

(2) Under these circumstances a Summons should be prepared and served on the taxpayer-boxholder in an attempt to secure information as to the contents of the box and to gain access. If this action does not accomplish the desired results, a writ of entry should be sought or a suit requested to open the safe deposit box.

Figure 4.9   Currently Not Collectible Accounts

5610

Determination of Currently Not Collectible Taxes

5611

General
(1) A Collection employee may determine that the accounts are currently not collectible.
(2) Reporting an account currently not collectible does not abate the assessment. It only stops current efforts to collect it. Collection can start again any time before the statutory period for collection expires.

5632

Unable-To-Pay Cases—Hardship

5632.1

General
(1) If collection of the liability would prevent the taxpayer from meeting necessary living expenses, it may be reported currently not collectible under a hardship closing code. Sometimes accounts should be reported currently not collectible even though the Collection Information Statement (CIS) shows assets or sources of income subject to levy.
   (a) [The Manual] provides guidelines for analyzing the taxpayer's financial condition.
   (b) Since each taxpayer's circumstances are unique, other factors such as age and health must be considered as appropriate.
   (c) Document and verify the taxpayer's financial condition.
   (d) Consider the collection potential of an offer in compromise.
(2) Consider an installment agreement before reporting an account currently not collectible as hardship.

Figure 4.10   Offers in Compromise

5712

Grounds for Compromise

5712.1

General Guidelines

The compromise of a tax liability can only rest upon doubt as to liability, doubt as to collectibility, or doubt as to both liability and collectibility. IRC 7122 does not confer authority to compromise tax, interest, or penalty where the liability is clear and there is no doubt as to the ability of the Government to collect. To compromise there must be room for mutual concessions involving either or both doubt as to liability or doubt as to ability to pay. This rules out, as ground for compromise, equity or public policy considerations peculiar to a particular case, individual hardships, and similar matters which do not have a direct bearing on liability or ability to pay.

5713.2

Advising Taxpayers of Offer Provisions

(1) When criminal proceedings are not contemplated and an analysis of taxpayer's assets, liabilities, income and expenses shows that a liability cannot realistically be paid in full in the foreseeable future, the collection potential of an offer in compromise should be considered. While it is difficult to outline the exact circumstances when an offer would be the appropriate collection tool, the existence of any of the following should govern offer consideration.

  (a) Liquidation of assets and payments from present and future income will not result in full payment of tax liability.

  (b) A non-liable spouse has property which he/she may be interested in utilizing to secure a compromise of spouse's tax debt.

  (c) The taxpayer has an interest in assets against which collection action cannot be taken. For example, the taxpayer who owes a separate liability, has an interest in property held in "tenancy by the entirety" which cannot be reached or subjected to the Notice of Federal Tax Lien because of the provisions of state law. Under the compromise procedures, the taxpayer's interest is included in the total assets available in arriving at an acceptable offer in compromise.

  (d) The taxpayer has relatives or friends who may be willing to lend or give the taxpayer funds for the sole purpose of reaching a compromise with the Service.

5721

General

The offer in compromise is the taxpayer's written proposal to the Government and, if accepted, is an agreement enforceable by either party under the law of

Figure 4.10 Offers in Compromise (Continued)

contracts. Therefore, it must be definite in its terms and conditions, since it directly affects the satisfaction of the tax liability.

5723.1

Prescribed Form

A taxpayer seeking to compromise a tax liability based on doubt as to collectibility must submit Form 433, Statement of Financial Condition and Other Information. This form includes questions geared to develop a full and complete description of the taxpayer's financial situation.

5723.3

Refusal To Submit Financial Statement

If a taxpayer professing inability to pay refuses to submit the required Form 433, the offer will be immediately rejected since the Service cannot determine whether the amount offered is also the maximum amount collectible.

5725.1

Liability of Husband and Wife

(1) Under IRC 6013(d)(3), the liability for income tax on a joint return by husband and wife is expressly made "joint and several." Either or both of the spouses are liable for the entire amount of the tax shown on a joint return. When the liability of both parties is sought to be compromised, the offer should be submitted in the names of and signed by both spouses in order to make the waiver and other provisions of the offer form effective against both parties.

(2) An "innocent spouse" may be relieved of liability in certain cases under IRC 6013(e) and IRC 6653(b). In the event that one of the jointly liable taxpayers claims to be an "innocent spouse," the question should be referred to the district Examination function for determination.

   (a) Should the offer be acceptable, the report should not be prepared until after the district Examination function has made its determination. Since a favorable decision for the party claiming "innocent spouse" will change the amount of the liability sought to be compromised, any recommendation for acceptance must reflect the redetermined liability.

5740

Investigation of Offers

5741.1

General

(1) Once an offer in compromise is received in Special Procedures function, a determination whether the offer merits further consideration must be made. SPf should use all information contained in the offer file and may consult with the revenue officer assigned the TDAs [tax deficiency

Figure 4.10 Offers in Compromise (Continued)

assessments] to obtain additional financial information or verify existing information.

(2) Summary rejection in SPf can be made on the grounds that the offer is frivolous, was filed merely to delay collection, or where there is no basis for compromise. A desk review of the offer can result in this determination. Although not all-inclusive, the following list provides guidelines on the criteria for summary rejection most often encountered:

    (a) Taxpayer has equity in assets subject to the Federal tax lien clearly in excess of the total liability sought to be compromised,

    (b) The total liability is extremely large and the taxpayer has offered only a minimum sum well below his/her equity and earning potential (e.g., offering $100 to compromise a $50,000 tax liability). Although the taxpayer could be persuaded to raise the offer, the fact that this initial amount offered was so low indicates bad faith and the desire to delay collection,

    (c) The taxpayer is not current in his/her filing or payment requirements for periods not included in the offer,

    (d) The taxpayer refuses to submit a complete financial statement (Form 433),

    (e) Acceptance of the offer would adversely affect the image of the government,

    (f) Taxpayer has submitted a subsequent offer which is not significantly different from a previously rejected offer and the taxpayer's financial condition has not changed,

    (g) In cases involving doubt as to liability for the 100-percent penalty, the liability is clearly established and the taxpayer has offered no new evidence to cast doubt on its validity.

5741.2

Public Policy

(1) An accepted offer, like any contract, is an agreement between two parties resulting from a "meeting of the minds." It is incumbent upon each party to negotiate the best terms possible. Normally, the offer and subsequent negotiations are of a private nature. However, when accepting an offer, the Service is in a unique position since it represents the government's interest in the negotiations and the accepted offer becomes part of public record. Therefore, public policy dictates that an offer can be rejected if public knowledge of the agreement is detrimental to the government's interest. The offer may be rejected even though it can be shown conclusively that the amounts offered are greater than could reasonably be collected in any other manner. Because the Government would be in the position of foregoing revenue, the circumstances in which public policy considerations could be used to reject the offer must be construed very strictly. The following may be used as a guideline for instances where public policy issues are most often encountered:

Figure 4.10   Offers in Compromise (Continued)

(a) Taxpayer's notoriety is such that acceptance of an offer will hamper future Service collection and/or compliance efforts. However, simply because the taxpayer is famous or well-known is not a basis in and of itself for rejecting the offer on public policy grounds.

(b) There is a possibility of establishing a precedent which might lead to numerous offers being submitted on liabilities incurred as a result of occupational drives to enforce tax compliance.

(c) Taxpayer has been recently convicted of tax related crimes. Again, the notoriety of the individual should be considered when making a public policy determination. The publicity surrounding the case, taxpayer's compliance since the case was concluded, or the taxpayer's position in the community should all be considered prior to rejecting an otherwise acceptable offer.

(d) Situations where it is suspected that the financial benefits of criminal activity are concealed or the criminal activity is continuing would normally preclude acceptance of the offer for public policy reasons. Criminal Investigation function should be contacted to coordinate the Government's action in these cases.

5

Bankruptcy for Wage Earners— A Positive Option

In these difficult economic times, all forms of bankruptcy filings have increased dramatically. However, many people are unaware of the Wage Earner Plan and how it can work to help them. The Wage Earner Plan allows individuals the same opportunity that the largest corporations enjoy—reorganization. The Wage Earner Plan was designed by Congress to allow individuals to reorganize their debts without losing all of their assets, as is the case in a bankruptcy filed under Chapter 7 of the Bankruptcy Code.

Many people may feel that they will be stigmatized or embarrassed by a bankruptcy filing. That attitude simply is not justified. A casual review of your daily newspaper will reveal that some of the largest corporations, prominent entertainers, sports figures and even attorneys have used the bankruptcy laws to put themselves back on level ground. Obviously, they did not feel stigmatized. Even though bankruptcy is a public matter, you would be surprised at how many of your neighbors are benefitting from a bankruptcy.

Conceptually and in practice, a Wage Earner Plan is uncomplicated. It is a court-sanctioned approach to sound debt management, i.e., living within an allowance by developing a budget.

A Wage Earner Plan provides you with many of the benefits of debt consolidation without the detriments of loans. Those benefits include:

- During the term of the plan, there are generally no interest charges for pre-existing debts.

- With the approval of the Court, you establish the amount you are willing and able to pay periodically to creditors.

- With the approval of the Court, you determine the amount your creditors will receive under the plan.

How the Process Works

A Wage Earner Plan or Chapter 13 case is launched with the filing of a Bankruptcy Petition. The petition, which is a disclosure form that shows the Court how you have budgeted your living expenses and how you propose to repay your creditors, is filed with the Clerk of the Bankruptcy Court. The form will contain your personal financial statement and show the portion of your income that is available to pay creditors after your living expenses are paid.

The commencement of any bankruptcy case stops all collection actions dead in their tracks. Further, other than support obligations, any wage attachments or garnishments are invalidated. All future payments to creditors will be made by your court-appointed trustee.

Shortly after the filing of your petition, you must attend a meeting of your creditors conducted by the trustee. This meeting will take place from one to six months after the filing of the petition. At the meeting the trustee will ask you, under oath, about your petition and your finances. It is the trustee's responsibility to determine the likelihood of a successful reorganization.

If the trustee determines that the plan has a likelihood of success, he or she will recommend that the judge confirm the plan. At this point you will meet with the judge, and the plan will be effective upon confirmation.

Who Can Use a Chapter 13 Wage Earner Plan?

Section 103(e) of the Bankruptcy Code identifies the persons who may take advantage of a Chapter 13 Wage Earner Plan reorganization effort. You must be an individual "with regular income that owes, on the date of filing the petition, noncontingent, liquidated, unsecured debts of less than $100,000 and noncontingent, liquidated, unsecured debts of less than $350,000." Further, you must be an individual residing in or having a domicile in the United States, and you must have a regular income. The regular income requirement is satisfied if your "income is sufficiently stable and regular" for you to be able to make payments under the plan.

Determining the Chapter 13 Plan

The largest hurdle you will face in your Chapter 13 efforts is creating your payment plan. Remember, it is possible that some debts will be discharged without payment in full. The balancing task requires you to recognize that:

- In general, a Chapter 13 should be completed within three years; and
- All unsecured creditors must receive what they would have received had you chosen a Chapter 7 complete liquidation plan.

In determining your plan, first identify the property that is subject to the bankruptcy and the property that is exempt. *Exempt property* is defined by statute. You may choose either the amounts granted under the federal bankruptcy code or your state's exemptions. There is no rule of thumb. Each state's exemptions differ, and you must carefully check your state's law before choosing.

For example, as will be explained in Chapter 6, pension funds are not exempt from bankruptcy under federal law. However, some states grant an exemption to pensions, i.e., Pennsylvania. In contrast, New Jersey does not exempt pensions. Therefore, in a Pennsylvania bankruptcy, the value of your pension would not be included in determining the amount to be paid under the bankruptcy plan, while in New Jersey it would.

Having identified and elected the correct exemption, all other property you own is nonexempt. The value of your nonexempt property is the minimum that your plan must pay out. Remember, for a Chapter 13 to be *confirmed*, unsecured creditors must receive at least what they would have if you had liquidated your assets under Chapter 7.

Dischargeable Debts

Most of your debts are dischargeable in a Chapter 13 bankruptcy. Discharge means the debt is extinguished and completely satisfied. Not all of your debts are dischargeable; those that are include:

- child support and alimony;
- debts not disclosed in your bankruptcy filing;
- restitution that is ordered because of criminal activity;
- debts obtained through either fraud or deceit;
- debts resulting from willful or malicious injury;
- debts on which final payment is due after the final date of the plan;
- debts that are reaffirmed after the confirmation of the plan;
- penalties and fines due for tax liabilities;
- certain tax liabilities, such as employment taxes; and
- student loans.

In general, all other debts you may have incurred are dischargeable; they will be wiped out after your plan has been completed.

Some Questions Concerning Chapter 13

Q. How do Chapter 13 and Chapter 7 bankruptcies differ?

A. A Chapter 7 is a complete liquidation, whereas a Chapter 13 is a *reorganization* and workout of your debts. In a Chapter 7 you will lose all of your nonexempt property, which will be sold by the trustee. The proceeds will be given to your creditors, and you will be completely discharged of your debts. In a Chapter 13 you keep all of your assets, both exempt and nonexempt. Your plan will pay off all the debts to the extent that the court determines possible, and the remainder of your debts will be discharged.

Q. How often may I file for bankruptcy?

A. You may file a Chapter 7 bankruptcy only once in six years. A Chapter 13 may be filed repeatedly; however, there is a six-month waiting period required between filings.

Q. What are the Chapter 13 fees?

A. The filing fee is $120. Further, the trustee receives a fee equal to ten percent of the total payments paid under the plan. If your plan requires $20,000 in payments, the fees would be a $120 filing fee plus a $2,000 trustee fee for a total of $2,120.

Q. How long will a Chapter 13 plan last?

A. In general, a Wage Earner Plan runs for three years. The plan may last as long as five years and, if all debts can be paid in less time, the plan can be shorter than three years.

Q. Can I have too much debt to qualify for a Chapter 13?

A. Yes. If you have unsecured debts that are liquidated or noncontingent and they exceed $100,000, or if you have secured debts that are liquidated or noncontingent and they exceed $350,000, you will not be allowed to file a Chapter 13 bankruptcy.

Q. What happens to guarantees or cosigned debts?

A. First, we must distinguish between consumer debt and business debt. In general, if the debt is a consumer debt to be fully paid during the Chapter 13, the creditor will not go against the cosigner or guarantor. However, if the debt is a business debt or is a consumer debt that will not be fully paid under the plan, the creditor can make the cosigner pay.

Q. Will I lose any property by filing a Chapter 13 plan?

A. Normally, no. The idea of the plan is to grant you time to *catch up* on your obligations. Debts are paid from income you receive after the filing of the bankruptcy. You may, however, lose some property if your nonexempt property is valuable and you would not otherwise pay to your creditors what they would receive if you liquidated your property.

Q. Will my filing be public?

A. Yes. The filing of a bankruptcy is public record. Many legal newspapers and most general circulation newspapers will print a list of bankruptcies.

Q. Does my employer have to know that I filed for bankruptcy?

A. Generally, the court, through the trustee, will contact your employer to either verify your income or to make arrangements for the payment of your income directly to the trustee in order to make plan payments.

Q. Can I be fired or discriminated against by my employer for filing bankruptcy?

A. No. It is a crime for any employer to discriminate against individuals for filing bankruptcy. However, some bonded positions, like security guards, stock brokers and casino cashiers, may have some difficulty. In those circumstances, open and frank discussion with employers should satisfy any fears.

Q. Must I repay all of my debts?

A. No. You are required, subject to court approval, to repay only as much of your debt as your creditors would have received if you liquidated all of your nonexempt property.

Q. Should a husband and wife file a plan jointly?

A. If both husband and wife have significant debts, they should file a joint plan. The only requirement is that at least one of the couple must have sufficient income and that their joint debts not exceed the dollar limits. In some states—those that recognize tenants by the entireties—it may be beneficial not to file a joint plan. The entireties property may be exempt from the bankruptcy if only one spouse files, whereas it will be subject to the bankruptcy if both spouses file jointly.

Q. How does a Chapter 13 affect my credit history?

A. At first, the filing may result in a worsening of your credit rating. Remember, credit agencies will report the bankruptcy on your file for up to ten years. However, if your debts are substantially paid off under the plan, many creditors will take that into account and treat you as one who has rehabilitated his or her credit.

How To File a Plan by Yourself

You do not need to use an attorney to file a Chapter 13 bankruptcy. The bankruptcy is started with the filing of the petition (see forms attached) and the payment of the filing fee of $120. Petition and bankruptcy forms are generally the same throughout the United States; however, the local District court may have chosen its own style. Check with the clerk of your local Bankruptcy Court. Although the clerks do not give *legal* advice, they are usually helpful and will aid you in your efforts to comply with local requirements.

The procedure is quite straightforward:

- Get a set of bankruptcy forms from your local legal supply store or office stationery store. These forms usually come as preprinted packages that have the correct number of carbon copies included.

- You must type the forms. Neatness does count. The Clerk of the Court will not accept improperly completed forms. If you need additional space to complete a schedule, use white paper and title it with the same name as the form you are continuing. You can expect to complete most of the listed forms:

    - Voluntary petition

    - Chapter 13 statement

    - Chapter 13 plan and related schedules (check with the clerk to see if local forms are provided)

    - Address matrix sheet

- Deliver the forms with the filing fee of $120 to the Clerk of the Bankruptcy Court. The number of copies you will need is determined by the local court. Check with the clerk prior to wasting a trip to court. Generally, five copies will be enough.

- The clerk will time-stamp a copy for you. This is your receipt. It should contain the case number assigned by the court; however, some courts are backlogged, and the clerk may not be able to issue your case number when you file. If this happens, contact the court within a few days to get your case number.

- If you are subject to a garnishment, contact both your employer and the creditor attaching your wages as soon as you have made your filing. The filing stops all forms of collection during the bankruptcy. A creditor may be held in contempt for trying to collect after being notified of the bankruptcy.

- Keep your case number handy. The court will notify your creditors, but you can speed things along by advising your creditors and collection agencies of your bankruptcy. They will need your case number.

- Keep the court advised of your address in the event that you move. Now you just have to wait for the process to go forward. Good Luck!

Figure 5.1 Property Exemptions under the Federal Bankruptcy Act and Other Federal Laws

**PROPERTY EXEMPTIONS
UNDER THE FEDERAL
BANKRUPTCY ACT**

TYPE OF PROPERTY EXEMPTED	STATUTES CREATING THE EXEMPTIONS	MAXIMUM AMOUNT EXEMPTED
Real or Personal Property used as a residence (includes Mobile Home) or a Burial Plot.	11 U.S.C. §522(d)(1)	$7,500.00
One Motor Vehicle.	11 U.S.C. §522(d)(2)	1,200.00
All items of household furnishings, goods and appliances.	11 U.S.C. §522(d)(3) (per item)* (See No. 1 below)	200.00
All items of wearing apparel.	11 U.S.C. §522(d)(3) (per item)* (See No. 1 below)	200.00
All items of: Books, Animals, Crops or Musical Instruments	11 U.S.C. §522(d)(3) (per item)* (See No. 1 below)	200.00
Jewelry (total value of all pieces)	11 U.S.C. §522(d)(4)	500.00
Professional Books, Tools of Trade and Implements	11 U.S.C. §522(d)(6)	750.00
Professionally prescribed Health Aids.	11 U.S.C. §522(d)(9)	any amount
Social Security Benefits, Unemployment Compensation, Public Assistance, Veterans Benefits, Alimony, Support, Separate Maintenance, Payments under a Stock Plan, Profit Sharing Plan, Annuity or other plan for the reason of illness, disability, death, age or length of service.	11 U.S.C. §522(d)(10)	any amount
An Award under the Crime Victims Reparation Law	11 U.S.C. §522(11)(A)	any amount
Life Insurance payments when debtor is the dependent of the insured.	11 U.S.C. §522(d)(11)(C)	any amount
A payment for the wrongful death of an individual of whom debtor was a dependent.	11 U.S.C. §522(d)(11)(B)	any amount
A payment for loss of future earnings of a debtor or an individual upon who debtor is dependent	11 U.S.C. §522(d)(11)(E)	any amount
Debtor's interest in any other property not particularly itemized in this Schedule	11 U.S.C. §522(d)(5)* (See No. 2 below)	400.00
A portion of the amounts not used under Section 522(d)(1) above to exempt Real or Personal property used as a residence or burial plot may be used under this statute to exempt any other property whether or not such property has been previously claimed under a previous statute.[2]	11 U.S.C. §522(d)(5)* (See No. 2 below)	3,750.00

NOTE: Under the 1984 amendments to the Bankruptcy Code, husband and wife debtors cannot claim separate exemptions under both the Federal Exemption Laws and the State Statutes. In other words, they must both claim their exemptions under the same set of laws. This is, of course, assuming that the Federal Exemption Laws apply in the State where you plan to file your action

[1]The maximum amount that can be exempted under this Section 522(d)(3) is an aggregate total of $4,000.00.

[2]Under this statute, any amount left over (not exceeding $3,750.00) after applying the allowed exemption to a residence or burial plot can be used to exempt other property whether previously exempted or not scheduled. For example, Boats, Airplanes, Income tax refunds, exempt wages, etc.

Figure 5.1 Property Exemptions under the Federal Bankruptcy Act and Other Federal Laws (Continued)

Exempt Property Under Other Federal Laws

There are various Federal Laws, other than the Federal Bankruptcy Laws, that provide for the exemption of certain property. These exemptions, as scheduled below, can be used in a Bankruptcy Action if there does not exist an applicable State or Federal Bankruptcy Exemption Statute which specifically exempts the possessed property. An example of this application is: (1) Income received under the Social Security Act, (2) Railroad Retirement Act, (3) Federal Civil Service Retirement Act, etc.

Property Exempted	Federal Statute
The earnings of a debtor subject to process is limited to a maximum of 25% of disposable earnings.	15 U.S.C. § 1673
Railroad Employees Retirement Benefits under the Railroad Retirement Act.	45 U.S. C. § 228(L)

Property Exempted	Federal Statute
All lands acquired by Federal Homestead Laws.	43 U.S.C. § 175
All Veterans Administration proceeds, including Veterans pensions, U.S. Life Insurance Benefits, pensions and disability allowances.	38 U.S.C. § 3101
Any and all benefits under the Social Security Act.	42 U.S.C. § 407
Retirement benefits under the Federal Civil Service or Employees Retirement Fund.	5 U.S.C. § 8346

Chapter 13 Petition and Schedules

Figure 5.2 Chapter 13 Voluntary Petition & Exhibit B

UNITED STATES BANKRUPTCY COURT FOR THE   DISTRICT OF

Date Petition Filed _____
Case Number _____
Bankruptcy Judge _____

In re

Debtor*

} CHAPTER 13
VOLUNTARY PETITION
& EXHIBIT "B"

Soc. Sec. No.   Debtor's Employer's Tax Id. No.

(If this form is used for joint petitioners wherever the word "petitioner" or words referring to petitioner are used they shall be read as if in the plural.)

1. Petitioner's mailing address, including county, is

2. Petitioner has
   - ☐ resided within this district for the preceding 180 days.
   - ☐ had his(*her*) domicile within this district for the preceding 180 days.
   - ☐ had his(*her*) principal place of business within this district for the preceding 180 days.
   - ☐ had his(*her*) principal assets within this district for the preceding 180 days.
   - ☐ resided or been domiciled or had his(*her*) principal place of business within this district for a longer portion of the preceding 180 days than in any other district.

3. Petitioner is qualified to file this petition and is entitled to the benefits of title 11, United States Code as a voluntary debtor.

4. ☐ A copy of petitioner's proposed plan, dated   19   is attached.
   ☐ Petitioner intends to file a plan pursuant to chapter 13 of title 11, United States Code.

5. A declaration in the form of Exhibit "B" is attached to and made a part of this petition.[1]

Wherefore, petitioner prays for relief in accordance with chapter 13 of title 11, United States Code.

Petitioner(s) signs if not represented by attorney

Signed: _____
           Attorney for Petitioner

Address: _____

_____

_____
Petitioner

_____
Petitioner

DECLARATION

INDIVIDUAL: I,   the petitioner named in the foregoing petition, declare under penalty of perjury under the laws of the United States that the foregoing is true and correct.

JOINT INDIVIDUALS: We,   and   the petitioners named in the foregoing petition, declare under penalty of perjury under the laws of the United States that the foregoing is true and correct.

Executed on   19   Signature: _____
                                        Petitioner

_____
Petitioner

EXHIBIT "B"

I,   the attorney for the petitioner named in the foregoing petition, declare that I have informed the petitioner that he or she may proceed under chapter 7 or 13 of title 11, United State Code, and have explained the relief available under each such chapter.

_____
Executed on

_____
Signature of Attorney for Petitioner

*Set forth here all names including tradenames used by Debtor within last 6 years.

[1]This paragraph applies if petitioner is an individual whose debts are primarily consumer debts and petitioner is represented by an attorney, otherwise delete.

Figure 5.3 Chapter 13 Statement

UNITED STATES BANKRUPTCY COURT FOR THE   DISTRICT OF   *Case No.*

In re

}
CHAPTER 13
STATEMENT

Debtor*

Soc. Sec. No.   Debtor's Employer's Tax Id. No.

(If this form is used by joint debtors wherever the word "debtor" or words referring to debtor are used they shall be read as if in the plural.)

Each question shall be answered or the failure to answer explained. If the answer is "none" or "not applicable" so state. If additional space is needed for the answer to any question, a separate sheet, properly identified and made a part hereof, should be used and attached.

The term, "original petition," used in the following questions, shall mean the original petition filed under § 301 of the Code or, if the chapter 13 case was converted from another chapter of the Code, shall mean the petition by or against you which originated the first case.

This form must be completed in full whether a single or a joint petition is filed. When information is requested for "each" or "either spouse filing a petition" it should be supplied for both when a joint petition is filed.

1. **Name and residence**   *(b)* Where does debtor, if single, or each spouse filing a petition now reside?   (3) Telephone number
   (a) Give full name   (1) Mailing address, (2) City or town, state and zip code   including area code

   Husband [or, *if single*, Debtor]

   Wife

   (c) What does debtor, if single, or each spouse filing a petition consider his or her residence, if different from that listed in (b) above?

        Husband [*or* Debtor]

        Wife

2. **Occupation and income** *(a)* Give present occupation of debtor, if single, or each spouse filing a petition. (If more than one, list all for debtors or each spouse filing a petition.)

        Husband [*or* Debtor]

        Wife

   (b) What is the name, address, and telephone number of present employer (or employers) of debtor, if single, or each spouse filing a petition? (Include also any identifying badge or card number with employer.)

        Husband [*or* Debtor]

        Wife

   (c) How long has debtor, if single, or each spouse filing a petition been employed by present employer?

        Husband [or Debtor]   Wife

   (d) If debtor or either spouse filing a petition has not been employed by present employer for a period of 1 year, state the name of prior employer(s) and nature of employment during that period.

        Husband [*or* Debtor]

        Wife

   (e) Has debtor or either spouse filing a petition operated a business, in partnership or otherwise, during the past 3 years? (If so, give the particulars, including names, dates, and places.)

        Husband [*or* Debtor]

        Wife

Figure 5.3 Chapter 13 Statement (Continued)

(f) Answer the following questions for debtor, if single, or each spouse whether single or joint petition is filed unless spouses are separated and a single petition is filed:

(1) What are your gross wages, salary or commissions per pay period?

	Husband [or Debtor]	Wife
(a) Weekly	$ _____	$ _____
(b) Semi-monthly	$ _____	$ _____
(c) Monthly	$ _____	$ _____
(d) Other (specify)	$ _____	$ _____

(2) What are your payroll deductions per pay period for:

	Husband [or Debtor]	Wife
(a) Payroll taxes (including social security)	$ _____	$ _____
(b) Insurance	$ _____	$ _____
(c) Credit union	$ _____	$ _____
(d) Union dues	$ _____	$ _____
(e) Other (specify)	$ _____	$ _____
(f) _____	$ _____	$ _____
(g) _____	$ _____	$ _____

(3) What is your take-home pay per period? Husband [or Debtor]$_____   Wife $_____

(4) What was the amount of your gross income for the last calendar year? Husband [or Debtor] $_____   Wife $_____

(5) Is your employment subject to seasonal or other change? Husband [or Debtor] $_____   Wife $_____

(6) Has either of you made any wage assignments or allotments? (If so, indicate which spouse's wages assigned or allotted, the name and address of the person to whom assigned or allotted, and the amount owing, if any, to such person. If allotment or assignment is to a creditor, the claim should also be listed in Item 11a.)

3. **Dependents** (To be answered by debtor if unmarried, otherwise for each spouse whether single or joint petition is filed unless spouses are separated and a single petition is filed.)

(a) Does either of you pay [or receive] alimony, maintenance or support?   If so, how much per month?
For whose support? (Give name, age, and relationship to you.)

Husband [or Debtor]

Wife

(b) List all other dependents, other than present spouse, not listed in (a) above. (Give name, age, and relationship to you.)

Husband [or Debtor]

Wife

Figure 5.3 Chapter 13 Statement (Continued)

4. Budget (a) Give your estimated average future monthly income if unmarried, otherwise for each spouse whether single or joint petition is filed, unless spouses are separated and a single petition is filed.

(1) Husband's (or Debtor's) monthly take-home pay _____ $ _____

(2) Wife's monthly take-home pay _____ $ _____

(3) Other monthly income (specify) _____ $ _____

(4) _____ $ _____

(5) _____ $ _____

(6) _____ $ _____

(7) _____ Total $ _____

(b) Give estimated average future monthly expenses of family (not including debts to be paid under plan), consisting of:

(1) Rent or home mortgage payment (include lot rental for trailer) _____ $ _____

(2) Utilities (Electricity $ _____ Heat $ _____ Water $ _____ Telephone $ _____) $ _____

(3) Food _____ $ _____

(4) Clothing _____ $ _____

(5) Laundry and cleaning _____ $ _____

(6) Newspapers, periodicals, and books (including school books) _____ $ _____

(7) Medical and drug expenses _____ $ _____

(8) Insurance (not deducted from wages): (a) Auto $ _____ (b) Other $ _____ _____ $ _____

(9) Transportation (not including auto payments to be paid under plan) _____ $ _____

(10) Recreation _____ $ _____

(11) Dues, union, professional, social or otherwise (not deducted from wages) _____ $ _____

(12) Taxes (not deducted from wages) _____ $ _____

(13) Alimony, maintenance, or support payments _____ $ _____

(14) Other payments for support of dependents not living at home _____ $ _____

(15) Other (specify): _____ $ _____

_____ $ _____

_____ $ _____

_____ $ _____

_____ $ _____

_____ $ _____

_____ Total $ _____

(c) Excess of estimated future monthly income (last line of Item 4(a) above) over estimated future exp. (last line of Item 4(b) above) _____ $ _____

(d) Total amount to be paid each month under plan _____ $ _____

5. Payment of attorney

(a) How much have you agreed to pay or what property have you agreed to transfer to your attorney in connection with this case? _____ $ _____

(b) How much have you paid or what have you transferred to the attorney? _____ $ _____

6. Tax refunds* To what tax refunds (income or other), if any, is either of you, or may either of you be entitled? (Give particulars, including information as to any refunds payable jointly to you or any other person. All such refunds should also be listed in Item 13(b).)

Figure 5.3 Chapter 13 Statement (Continued)

7. **Financial accounts, certificates of deposit and safe deposit boxes***

    (a) Does either of you currently have any accounts or certificates of deposit or shares in banks, savings and loan, thrift, building and loan and homestead associations, credit unions, brokerage houses, pension funds and the like? (If so, give name and address of each institution, number and nature of account, current balance, and name and address of every other person authorized to make withdrawals from the account. Such accounts should also be listed in Item 13(b).)

    (b) Does either of you currently keep any safe deposit boxes or other depositories? (If so, give name and address of bank or other depository, name and address of every other person who has a right of access thereto, and a brief description of the contents thereof, which should also be listed in Item 13(b).)

8. **Prior Bankruptcy** What proceedings under the Bankruptcy Act or Bankruptcy Code have previously been brought by or against you or either spouse filing a petition? (State the location of the bankruptcy court, the nature and number of each proceeding, the date when it was filed, and whether a discharge was granted or denied, the proceeding was dismissed, or a composition, arrangement, or plan was confirmed.)

9. **Foreclosures, executions, and attachments*** (a) Is any of the property of either of you, including real estate, involved in a foreclosure proceeding, in or out of court? (If so, identify the property and the person foreclosing.)

    (b) Has any property or income of either of you been attached, garnished, or seized under any legal or equitable process within the 90 days immediately preceding the filing of the original petition herein? (If so, describe the property seized, or person garnished, and at whose suit.)

10. **Repossessions and returns*** Has any property of either of you been returned to, repossessed, or seized by the seller or by any other party, including a landlord, during the 90 days immediately preceding the filing of the original petition herein? (If so, give particulars, including the name and address of the party taking the property and its description and value.)

Figure 5.3 Chapter 13 Statement (Continued)

11. **Transfers of Property*** *(a)* Has either of you made any gifts, other than ordinary and usual presents to family members and charitable donations, during the year immediately preceding the filing of the original petition herein? (If so, give names and addresses of donees and dates, description and value of gifts.)

    (b) Has either of you made any other transfer, absolute or for the purpose of security, or any other disposition, of real or personal property during the year immediately preceding the filing of the original petition herein? (Give a description of the property, the date of the transfer or disposition, to whom transferred or how disposed of, and, if the transferee is a relative or insider, the relationship, the consideration, if any, received therefor, and the disposition of such consideration.)

12. **Debts** (To be answered by debtor, if unmarried, otherwise for each spouse whether single or joint petition is filed.)

    (a) *Debts Having Priority.*

(1) Nature of claim	(2) Name of creditor and complete mailing address, including zip code	(3) Specify when claim was incurred and the consideration therefor: when claim is subject to setoff, evidenced by a judgment, negotiable instrument, or other writing	(4) Indicate if claim is contingent, unliquidated, or disputed	(5) M(D) W or J	(6) Amount of claim
1. Wages, salary, and commissions, including vacation, severance and sick leave pay owing to employees not exceeding $2,000 to each, earned within 90 days before filing of petition or cessation of business (if earlier specify date).					$
2. Contributions to employee benefit plans for services rendered within 180 days before filing of petition or cessation of business (if earlier specify date).					
3. Deposits by individuals, not exceeding $900 for each for purchase, lease, or rental of property or services for personal, family, or household use that were not delivered or provided.					
4. Taxes owing (itemize by type of tax and taxing authority) (A) To the United States (B) To any state (C) To any other taxing authority					
				Total	

    (b) *Secured Debts.*—List all debts which are or may be secured by real or personal property. (Indicate in sixth column, if debt payable in installments, the amount of each installment, the installment period (Monthly, weekly, or otherwise) and number of installments in arrears, if any. Indicate in the last column whether husband or wife solely liable, or whether you are jointly liable.)

Creditor's name, account number and complete mailing address, Including zip code	Consideration or basis for debt	Amount claimed by creditor	If disputed, amount admitted by debtor	Description of collateral (include year and make of automobile)	Installment amount, period, and number of installments in arrears	Husband or wife solely liable, or jointly liable

Total secured debts $ _____

Figure 5.3   Chapter 13 Statement (Continued)

12. **Debts** (Continued)

(c) *Unsecured Debts.*—List all other debts, liquidated and unliquidated, including taxes, attorneys' fees and tort claims.

Creditor's name, account number and complete mailing address, including zip code	Consideration or basis for debt	Amount claimed by creditor	If disputed, amount admitted by debtor	Husband or wife solely liable, or jointly liable

(a)	Total debts having priority	$	
(b)	Total secured debts	$	
(c)	Total unsecured debts	$	
	Total (a) + (b) + (c)	$	

13. **Codebtors** (To be answered by debtor, if unmarried, otherwise for each spouse whether single or joint petition is filed.)

(a) Are any other persons liable, as cosigners, guarantors or in any other manner, on any of the debts of either of you or is either of you so liable on the debts of others? (If so, give particulars, indicating which spouse liable and including names of creditors, nature of debt, names and addresses of codebtors, and their relationship, if any, to you.)

(b) If so, have the codebtors made any payments on the debts? (Give name of each codebtor and amount paid by codebtor.)

(c) Has either of you made any payments on the debts? (If so, specify total amount paid to each creditor, whether paid by husband or wife, and name of codebtor.)

Figure 5.3 Chapter 13 Statement (Continued)

14. **Property and Exemptions** (To be answered by debtor, if unmarried, otherwise for each spouse whether single or joint petition is filed.)

   (a) *Real Property.*—List all real property owned by either of you at date of filing of original petition herein. (Indicate in last column whether owned solely by husband of wife, or jointly.)

Description and location of property	Name of any co-owner other than spouse	Present market value (without deduction for mortgage or other security interest)	Amount of mortgage or other security interest on this property	Name of mortgage or other secured creditor	Value claimed exempt. (Specify federal or state statute creating the exemption)	Owned solely by husband or wife, or jointly

   (b) Personal Property.—List all other property owned by either of you at date of filing of original petition herein.

Description	Location of property if not at debtor's residence	Name of any co-owner other than spouse	Present market value (without deduction for mortgage or other security interest)	Amount of mortgage or other security interest on this property	Name of mortgage of other secured creditor	Value claimed exempt. (Specify federal or state statute creating the exemption)	Owned solely by husband or wife, or jointly
Auto (give year and make):							
Household goods:							
Personal effects:							
Cash or financial account:							
Other (specify):							

Unsworn Declaration under Penalty of Perjury
(To be signed by both spouses when joint petition is filed.)

I (*We*) _____ and _____ declare under penalty of perjury under the laws of the United States that I (*we*) have read the answers contained in the foregoing statement, consisting of _____ sheets, and that they are true and complete to the best of my (*our*) knowledge, information, and belief.

Executed on _____ 19_____

_____   _____
Signature Husband (or Debtor)   Signature (Wife)

Attorney for Debtors & Address _____

Figure 5.4 Chapter 13 Plan

UNITED STATES BANKRUPTCY COURT FOR THE _____ DISTRICT OF _____   Case No.

In re _____

} CHAPTER 13
   PLAN

Debtor, Soc. Sec. No. _____
[Include here all names used by debtor within last 6 years.]

(If this form is used by joint debtors wherever the word "debtor" or words referring to debtor are used they shall be read as if in the plural.)

1. The future earnings of the debtor are submitted to the supervision and control of the trustee and the [*debtor — debtor's employer*] shall pay to the trustee the sum of $ _____ *weekly — bi-weekly — semi-monthly — monthly.*

2. › From the payments so received, the trustee shall make disbursements as follows:

   (a) The priority payments required by 11 U.S.C. §507.

   (b) After the above payments, dividends to secured creditors whose claims are duly proved and allowed as follows:

   (c) *Subsequent to — pro rata with* dividends to secured creditors, dividends to unsecured creditors whose claims are duly proved and allowed as follows:

3. The following executory contracts of the debtor are rejected:

    Title to the debtor's property shall revest in the debtor *on confirmation of a plan — upon dismissal of the case after confirmation pursuant to 11 U.S.C. §1329 — upon closing of the case pursuant to 11 U.S.C. §350.*

Dated: _____   _____   _____
                          Debtor   *Debtor*

Acceptances may be mailed to _____   _____
                                                Post Office Address

Figure 5.5 Chapter 13 Plan Worksheet

BANKRUPT NAME & ADDRESS	ATTORNEY(S) NAME & ADDRESS	BANKRUPT/DEBTOR NO.
DISTRICT DIRECTOR INTERNAL REVENUE SERVICE DISTRICT OFFICE ADDRESS	START A-Z LIST OF CREDITORS	

DO NOT TYPE IN THIS AREA

If a debt is disclosed to the United States other than one for taxes, type an address for the United States Attorney for the district in which the case is pending and to the department, agent or instrumentality of the United States through which the bankrupt became indebted.

Check with your local district for addresses of state or local government agencies to which addressed label must be prepared.

Figure 5.6 Schedule of Current Income and Current Expenditures

UNITED STATES BANKRUPTCY COURT FOR THE _____ DISTRICT OF _____ Case No. _____

In re _____

Soc. Sec. No. _____ Debtor's Employer's Tax Id. No. _____ Debtor*

} SCHEDULE OF CURRENT INCOME AND CURRENT EXPENDITURES

If this form is used by joint debtors wherever the question requires separate answers for Husband (H), Wife (W) or Joint (J) insert the appropriate symbol in column headed H, W or J.

Current Income

A. Give your current monthly income if unmarried, otherwise for each spouse whether single or joint petition is filed, unless spouses are separated and a single petition is filed.

H, W or J

(1) Debtor's monthly take-home pay _____ ___ $ _____
(2) Spouse's monthly take-home pay _____ ___ $ _____
(3) Regular income available from operation of a business or profession _____ ___ $ _____
(4) Do you receive alimony, maintenance or support payments?
    If so, state monthly amount _____ ___ $ _____
    State the name, age and relationship to you of persons for whose benefit payments are received
    _____
    _____
    _____
(5) Pension, social security or retirement income _____ ___ $ _____

(6) Other monthly income (specify) _____ ___ $ _____
    _____ ___ $ _____
    _____ ___ $ _____
    _____ ___ $ _____
    _____ ___ $ _____
                                                Total $ _____

Current Expenditures

B. Give current monthly expenditures of family, consisting of:

H, W or J

(1) Rent or home mortgage payment (include lot rental for trailer) _____ ___ $ _____
(2) (Electricity $ ___ Heat $ ___ Water $ ___ Telephone $ ___) ___ $ _____
(3) Food _____ ___ $ _____
(4) Clothing _____ ___ $ _____
(5) Laundry and cleaning _____ ___ $ _____
(6) Newspapers, periodicals, and books (including school books) _____ ___ $ _____
(7) Medical and drug expenses _____ ___ $ _____
(8) Insurance (not deducted from wages): (a) Auto $ ___ (b) Other $ ___ ___ $ _____
(9) Transportation _____ ___ $ _____
(10) Recreation _____ ___ $ _____
(11) Dues, union, professional, social or otherwise (not deducted from wages) _____ ___ $ _____
(12) Taxes (not deducted from wages) _____ ___ $ _____
(13) Alimony, maintenance, or support payments _____ ___ $ _____
    State the name, age and relationship to you of persons for whose benefit payments are made
    _____
    _____
(14) Other payments for support of dependents not living at home _____ ___ $ _____
(15) Expenditures deducted from wages (specify) _____ ___ $ _____
    _____ ___ $ _____
    _____ ___ $ _____
    _____ ___ $ _____
(16) Other (specify) _____ ___ $ _____
    _____ ___ $ _____
    _____ ___ $ _____
    _____ ___ $ _____
    _____ ___ $ _____
                                                Total $ _____

*Set forth here all names including tradenames used by Debtor within last 6 years.

6

Retirement, Income, Homestead and Other Exemption Protection

Most people concerned with asset protection—especially those who have incurred significant debt—are unaware that federal and state laws have been enacted to protect two of their most significant assets. Retirement plans and homes usually represent the primary portion of a person's wealth. The protection granted by law creates specific exemptions for retirement plans and homes, as well as insurance, wages and other forms of income. This chapter will examine these exemptions in detail.

Retirement and Pension Plans

Retirement and pension plans should be analyzed from the aspect of *qualified pension plans* and all other retirement plans, i.e., Individual Retirement Accounts, Governmental Pensions and Individual Retirement Annuities.

Qualified retirement plans (the private pension system) are governed by the Employee Retirement Income Security Act of 1974 (ERISA). ERISA was enacted to protect the rights of employees (and their beneficiaries) enrolled in benefit plans sponsored by their employers or union. Before ERISA it was not unusual for employees to retire assuming they would receive pension payments only to find that there were no funds available for retirement.

In order to be a qualified pension plan, a retirement plan must satisfy all of the provisions of ERISA, which was enacted specifically to protect the retirement funds of employees. A key ERISA requirement states that the plan must be a spendthrift trust if it is to qualify. Under the federal law, a spendthrift trust is one that prohibits its beneficiary from pledging or in any way "alienating" the principal or income of the plan.

If a plan qualifies, neither its income nor its principal can be reached by the beneficiary's creditors. Section 401(a)(13) of the Internal Revenue Code requires that benefits of a plan may not be subject to garnishment or execution. There are two major exceptions to this rule:

1. The prohibitions against attachment do not prevent the Internal Revenue Service from collecting federal tax liabilities from the plan, and

2. Parties to a divorce action may attach benefits through a "Qualified Domestic Relations Order" (QDRO).

A QDRO is a special domestic relations order that permits an "alternate payee" to obtain a portion or all of the benefits that the individual earning the pension would be entitled to receive. The statute recognizes the right of the alternate payee to be assigned and receive all or part of the individual participant's pension. The statute applies only to private pension plans governed by ERISA.

Under a QDRO, the alternate payee may be your spouse, child or any other dependent the local domestic relations court determines is someone to whom you owe a support obligation.

A QDRO must be a domestic relations order. It can be an order of the court, a consent decree entered by a domestic relations court or an order approving divorce settlements, which includes support, alimony or property division terms. It can not be issued by any court not authorized to handle domestic relation matters, i.e. small claims court or bankruptcy court.

A QDRO must include the name and mailing address of the individual who is covered by the pension plan and the name and mailing address of the alternate payee. It must state the dollar total of the pension or the ratio that the alternate payee is to receive. The pension plan will accept the QDRO if the addresses are missing, but only if the pension plan administrator has independent knowledge of the address. For example, if you are an officer in the company, the plan administrator would have your address as part of the company's payroll records.

In addition, once a QDRO is recognized by the pension plan, the QDRO will remain in force if a successor pension plan is adopted by the employer, i.e.—a plan that replaces the original plan of either your current employer or any successor employer who has adopted or taken over the original plan.

Ordinarily, a QDRO is issued to satisfy an individual's support or property obligation to an ex-spouse. A QDRO can also be an asset protection tool. A properly issued QDRO should not be subject to attack as a fraudulent transfer since it satisfies a legal obligation, and, as such it is a transfer for fair consideration. Further, creditors would not have the ability to attack the propriety of the QDRO, because it is exempt from an attachment by creditors (see discussion under bankruptcy). Therefore, you could enter into an order "assigning" your entire interest in your pension to your spouse, child or other dependent.

For example: Assume you now receive payments from your pension plan and your children are in college or are about to enter college. A QDRO could be issued on behalf of your children assigning them as much of the pension as is necessary to pay their college tuition and expenses. The remainder could be paid to your spouse. Since you now receive none of the pension, there is no money for your creditors to attach.

Further, the provisions of ERISA were written broadly in order to prevent a state court, other than by way of a QDRO, to order payments from a pension plan to creditors.

However, as participants in a pension plan, individuals may voluntarily assign a portion of their rights in the plan. This assignment must be voluntary, revocable and may not exceed ten percent of the benefit payment. Further, the individual must be in pay status (already receiving their pension payments)—in order to consent to the assignment. Levies, garnishments, executions or other nonvoluntary processes are not considered voluntary. Your creditors cannot obtain a court order requiring you to *voluntarily* assign your pension benefits.

This limitation on state courts was recently attacked successfully in one state court. That court breached the anti-alienation protection of ERISA by finding that the pension trust was not a spendthrift trust, as required by law. In order to find that the plan permitted its beneficiary to alienate his interest, the state court relied on state law principles. It pointed to the facts that the beneficiary in question was the:

- sole shareholder of the corporation that established the plan;

- only trustee of the plan; and

- sole beneficiary of the plan.

Under state (but not federal) law, these facts would support a finding that the plan was not a spendthrift plan.

There is one other situation in which the interest of a qualified plan's beneficiary may be reached by a creditor. Federal and state courts have also recognized an exemption to the anti-alienation rule based on an employee's fraud or criminal conduct against his or her employer. Again, this exemption has been very narrowly recognized, and when it is applied, only the employer can attack the beneficiary's interest in the plan.

Tip _____

Are you the sole trustee of a pension plan in which you are the sole beneficiary? Many states have held that a plan trust cannot exist if the beneficiary is the sole trustee of the plan. It is highly advisable to name more than one trustee. Similarly, a husband and wife co-trustee situation may be subject to attack in the state court. Choose an independent person to serve as your co-trustee.

Do you use the pension monies as your private bank account? Plan loans to only the owner of a business will invite scrutiny. DO NOT GO TO THE PLAN LIKE A SAVINGS ACCOUNT. Monies deposited are intended for retirement.

Do not be afraid to allow your plan to accumulate large amounts of money. Some creditors' attorneys have argued that creditors should be allowed to reach unreasonable accumulations. To date, this argument has fallen on deaf ears.

If your pension is attacked in state court allegedly because it is not a "spendthrift" trust, make certain your attorney is an expert in ERISA. The attorney should immediately try to move the issue to federal court. It is beyond the scope of this book to discuss litigation rules and strategies; however, a local judge is more apt to try to pierce the shield of a pension in order to protect a local citizen, than a federal judge who is more likely to construe ERISA strictly. Also, a federal judge usually has more experience in these issues and will not be swayed by the emotionalism of a fraud claim.

Bankruptcy

The Supreme Court recently removed any doubt as to the status of pension plan interests. The Court's holding "gives full and appropriate effect to ERISA's goal of protecting pension benefits." Pension benefits and interests in pension plans are excluded from an individual's bankruptcy estate. This protection covers only private pension plans governed by ERISA; it does not extend to Individual Retirement Accounts or Individual Retirement Annuities.

In light of the Supreme Court's determination that pension plans are exempt from bankruptcy and that IRAs receive only the limited, partial protection provided by state laws, you would be well advised to keep your retirement monies shielded in a qualified plan. Most individuals do not want to leave their pension monies behind when they leave an employer. However, if you take your money in a lump-sum distribution and either hold it or put it in an IRA, a creditor can reach and take the entire amount of your retirement nest egg.

Further, in the spring of 1992, Congress enacted the Unemployment Act, which allows individuals to take their pension monies with them and to ease the transferring of pension monies.

The Internal Revenue Code permits individuals to "roll-over" tax-free cash or other property received from one retirement plan to another. Amounts that are received from a qualified pension plan may be transferred to another qualified plan by way of a *conduit IRA*. To constitute a conduit IRA, the IRA must only hold assets that were distributed from a qualified plan. Further the second or recipient qualified plan must allow the acceptance of roll-over funds.

Therefore, it is recommended that you establish your own individual Keogh plan. However, all qualified plans must have a sponsor that is in business. Accordingly, you must be in business and reflect that by the necessary filings on your income tax return.

If you are already in business for yourself, you may transfer the funds to your plan, but first check to make certain that your plan will accept the rollover. If your plan does not, the amendment to correct the situation is not difficult, and the protection it affords is worthwhile.

Keogh Plans

If you are a participant in a Keogh plan that has multiple participants, the same principles that apply to qualified pension plans will apply to your Keogh plan. Generally, the plan is exempt from attachment by creditors and may even be exempt from creditors in bankruptcy.

A problem does arise in one-participant Keogh plans, which are not granted the same level of protection under ERISA. Many state courts have allowed attachment by creditors because:

- the funds may be withdrawn at will, and

- an individual cannot be the trustee of a spendthrift trust for his or her benefit.

Tip

If faced with this situation, look for a "friendly" co-trustee. The likelihood of a successful attack is greatly reduced when an independent trustee is responsible for the administration of the plan and trust. In this situation, it is probably safe to have your spouse serve as the co-trustee.

IRAs

There is no federal protection for IRAs. They are by their nature custodial accounts that are set aside for retirement. They do not have a separate trustee. However, many state statutes exempt all retirement funds from attachment. In a Pennsylvania case, a bank attached an IRA it held in order to pay off a defaulted loan. The court emphatically denied the bank the monies, stating that retirement funds were not to be touched.

Tip

Check your state's laws. If your particular state does not grant sanctuary to your retirement monies, consider transferring your IRA to a financial institution in a state that does protect such funds.

Social Security

Notwithstanding the fact that Social Security is not a pension for purposes of ERISA, Social Security payments of all types, including disability payments, are fully exempt from attachment by creditors.

Homestead Protection

Most states protect family homes from attachment by creditors. The *homestead exemption* provides protection for what is probably the most significant asset owned by most families. Under the exemption, the homeowner or family head is permitted to exempt the homestead from execution for general debts. Obviously, the exemption does not protect the property from mortgage foreclosure actions.

What Is a Homestead?

A homestead is the primary residence of the head of the family. The exemption is limited to one property. The residence, however, need not be a single-family home. It can be an apartment, a condominium or even undeveloped land.

Your state's statutes will provide the technical requirements for electing the exemption. It is clear, however, that the exemption attaches only to the primary residence. You, therefore, must carefully choose which property to protect if you have more than one homestead. A vacation home, for example, may have greater value than your *primary residence*. If you own more than one home, therefore, do not automatically assume that the dwelling place you use for the better part of the year should be categorized as your homestead.

Who Can Elect?

Generally, only one spouse can exercise the homestead exemption. For this reason, careful consideration should be given to the question of who should be deemed the head of the family for purposes of the exemption. The wisest course is to determine which spouse is most vulnerable to attack from creditors and to designate that person the head of the household. In many families today both spouses may be *breadwinners*, and there may not be a clear-cut answer to the question of which spouse is more vulnerable. One guideline that may help two-earner families resolve this question calls for the spouse who is self-employed to be deemed the head of the family. This approach recognizes the fact that a self-employed person usually runs greater financial risks than an employee.

Which Debts Are Exempt?

State law usually determines the precise nature of debts against which the homestead exemption applies and those against which it does not provide a shield. There are only two categories of debt to consider:

1. Debts you incurred before you purchased the property for which you seek the exemption, and

2. Those incurred after you purchased the property for which you seek the exemption.

Virtually every state will allow its exemption to shield the property from debts incurred after the purchase of the family home. The states are split, however, on how to apply the exemption with respect to debts incurred before the purchase of a home. Some states permit the exemption to protect the family home regardless of when the debt was incurred. Other states take a more restrictive position and do not enforce the exemption against debts incurred before the purchase of the family home.

How Much Protection Is Available?

Every state has its own rules governing the amount of the homestead exemption. In a few states, New Jersey, for example, your home is entirely unprotected. At the other extreme are states like Florida that shield your home against all debts (other than IRS debts), whatever their size and whenever they were incurred. Recent articles, in fact, have reported that large-wealth individuals have purchased multimillion dollar homes in Florida in order to take advantage of its generous homestead exemption.

Factors To Consider

The homestead exemption is not an all-in-one answer to asset protection needs. Ultimately, the election of the homestead exemption may not provide you with sufficient protection from creditors or for your home itself. However, the exemption is a valuable tool in your overall efforts to build a complete asset protection structure to shelter yourself and your family from attacks by creditors. When you review the homestead exemption as you build your asset protection program, you should consider the following potential problems:

- If your state's homestead exemption law does not exempt the entire value of your home from attack by creditors, a significant portion of your equity (the difference between your home's fair market value and the mortgage(s) on your home) may be exposed to risk.

- Even in states that allow the exemption to protect all of your equity in your home, the homestead exemption will not protect your home from attack by mortgagees or the IRS.

- In some states, the exemption may not protect your home against claims from creditors on debts that you incurred before you purchased your home.
- If you decide to sell or refinance your home after electing to exercise your homestead exemption, you may run into legal tangles. Although these tangles can be unknotted, it may take additional time to close on the refinancing or sale.

Tip

Given the financial and emotional significance of the asset in question—your home—you should consult an attorney familiar with your state's law to find out whether the homestead exemption applies to all debts, regardless of when they were incurred, the amount of the exemption and what you must do to ensure that you not lose this potentially vital form of protection.

Life Insurance

In today's society, life insurance can address many needs—protection for one's spouse or children, investment options and income stream. When the first exemptions for life insurance were drafted, state legislatures were concerned primarily with protecting the family of the insured. Today, all 50 states grant an exemption for life insurance whether purchased by the insured person individually or as part of a group plan.

States do differ in the amount of the exemption. Many states exempt all of the proceeds of the policy (as well as the cash surrender value of whole life polices) from creditors' claims. If a state's exemption provision is limited to a specific dollar amount, any amount above that limit is available to satisfy claims made by creditors of the insured. Similarly, a state's exemption provisions may cover the cash surrender value of whole life policies. If, however, the state sets a limit on the amount of the exemption, amounts above the limit on the cash surrender value of the policy may be reached by creditors.

The exemption also applies if the life insurance policy is investment sensitive. Various techniques have been adopted by insurance companies to make life insurance an investment designed to provide an income stream for the insured. It is possible that such policies will come under attack from creditors of the insured in the future. As of this writing, no state court appears to have denied the exemption to life insurance policies that have a substantial investment motive. You may want to consider the use of life insurance as part of your overall planning to protect your assets.

Maximizing Your Protection

In order to gain maximum protection from the exemption offered for life insurance, there are several factors that you should consider and act upon:

- If you are the beneficiary of a policy, some states will extend the exemption to you with respect to either all or a portion of the proceeds. In states that offer no such exemption or only limited protection, your creditors may be able to reach all or part of the proceeds.
- Even in states that extend the exemption to beneficiaries, you must be careful not to mingle insurance proceeds with other funds. If you permit commingling, you run the risk of losing the exemption.
- If your home state does not extend the exemption to beneficiaries, you may want to ask the insured person (or the owner of the policy if the owner is not the insured person) to create a trust and name it as the beneficiary of the policy and you as a beneficiary of the trust. Another option is to ask to have your spouse or children named as the beneficiaries of the policy.
- To maximize the protection of both the cash surrender value portion of your policy and the proceeds of the policy, consider creating an irrevocable life insurance trust. This step may also provide you with additional tax benefits.

Welfare Payments

Because it is offered to enable people in need to live at a subsistence level, Aid to Families with Dependent Children (AFDC) is granted an exemption from garnishment by at least half of the states in the country. Several states extend this exemption to other public assistance payments, such as those made to the blind, the disabled and the elderly. By the same token, nearly half of the states do not offer any exemption protection for public assistance funds.

In states where the exemption exists, most laws are worded so that the state cannot be garnished for payments to be made to recipients. In those states the exemptions also remain in place after the money is paid to the recipient. But, to ensure that creditors do not reach the payment after it has been made, the recipient should take care not to commingle public assistance payments with other monies they may have, since creditors may be able to reach a commingled fund.

Wages, Alimony, Child Support

Most states have taken the position that it is in the best interests of the public to exempt employees' wages from attachment by creditors. Some states go so far as to completely bar the attachment and garnishment of wages, e.g., Florida, Pennsylvania and Texas. Even in those states, however, the protection against attachment and garnishment does not extend to either child support or alimony payments.

Even if your state offers only limited protection against garnishment, there is a federal law that may protect your wages. The Consumer Credit Protection Act, a federal law, sets a maximum on the amount that can be garnished from your wages. The federal limit looks to the garnishee's disposable income, i.e., the amount left in your paycheck after federal and state withholding taxes and payments have been taken out. That limit is the lesser of:

- 25 percent of the garnishee's disposable income, or
- the amount by which the garnishee's disposable income exceeds 30 times the existing hourly federal minimum wage rate.

Like the state provisions, the Consumer Credit Protection Act does not apply to garnishments sought for child support or alimony payments ordered by a court.

The following Figure contains the income exemptions provided by each state.

Figure 6.1 State Homestead and Income Exemptions

State	Homestead Exemption	Amount Subject to Garnishments
Alabama	$5,000, not to exceed 160 acres of land. Alabama Cons. 6-10-2.	25% of earnings. Alabama Cons. 6-10-7.
Alaska	$54,000. Alaska Stat. 9.38.010	Earnings in excess of $350 per week. Alaska Stat. 9.38.030.
Arizona	$100,00, including traceable cash proceeds for 18 months after sale. Arizona Stat. 33-1101.	Lesser of amount in excess of 30 times federal minimum wage or 25% of earnings. Arizona Stat. 33-1131.
Arkansas	$2,500, but if outside of town at least 160 acres and at least 1/4 acre inside of town. Arkansas Stat. 16-66-210.	Earnings in excess of $25 per week for 60 days. Arkansas Stat. 16-66-208.
California	$75,000, increases to $100,000 if 65 or older or over 55 and disabled. California Cons. 704.730.	No exemption.
Colorado	$20,000 if owner occupied, including traceable proceeds for one year. Colorado Stat. 38-41-201.	Lesser of excess of 30 times federal minimum wage or 25% of earnings. Colorado Stat. 5-5-105.
Connecticut	None.	Greater of excess of 40 times federal minimum wage or 25% of earnings. Connecticut Stat. 52-361.
Delaware	None.	15% of earnings. 10 Delaware Code Annot. § 4913.
Florida	150 contiguous acres outside municipality or 1/2 acre inside municipality.	0% of earnings. Florida Stat. Annot. 222.11.

Figure 6.1 State Homestead and Income Exemptions (Continued)

Georgia	$5,000. Georgia Cons. Laws Annot. 44-13-1.	Lesser of excess of 30 times federal minimum wage or 25% of earnings. Georgia Cons. Laws Annot. 18-4-20.
Hawaii	$20,000; increased to $30,000 if over age 65 or head of household. Hawaii Stat. 651-92.	0% of earnings. Hawaii Stat. 651-121.
Idaho	$30,000. Idaho Cons. Laws 55-1003.	Lesser of excess of 30 times federal minimum wage or 25% of earnings. Idaho Cons. Laws 11-207.
Illinois	$7,500, including traceable proceeds for one year. Illinois Stat. Annot. 12-901.	Lesser of excess of 40 times federal minimum wage or 15% of gross earnings. Illinois Stat. Annot. 12-803.
Indiana	$7,500. Indiana Stat. 34-2-28-1.	Lesser of excess of 30 times federal minimum wage or 25% of earnings. Indiana Stat. 24-4.5-5-105.
Iowa	40 acres if not within city; 1/2 acre if within city; both at least $500 in value. Iowa Code 561-2.	Lesser of excess of 40 times federal minimum wage or 25% of earnings limited to no more than 10% of earnings. Iowa Code 642-21.
Kansas	160 acres of rural land; 1 acre in city. Kansas Stat. Annot. 60-2301.	Lesser of excess of 30 times federal minimum wage or 25% of earnings. Kansas Stat. Annot. 60-2310.
Kentucky	$5,000. Kentucky Stat. 427.060.	Lesser of excess of 30 times federal minimum wage or 25% of earnings. Kentucky Stat 427.010.
Louisiana	160 acres, not to exceed $15,000 in value. Louisiana Stat. Annot. 20:1.	Greater of excess of 30 times federal minimum wage or 25% of earnings. Louisiana Stat. Annot. 13:3881A.

Figure 6.1 State Homestead and Income Exemptions (Continued)

Maine	$7,500, increasing to $60,000 if over age 60 or disabled, with disabled dependent. Maine Stat. Annot. 4422.	100% of earnings.
Maryland	Only bankruptcy, then $2,500. Maryland Stat. 11-504	Lesser of amount in excess of $145 per week or 25% of earnings. Maryland Stat. 15-601.1.
Massachusetts	$100,000, but must be declared. Massachusetts Laws Annot. 188 § 1.	Lesser of 25% of earnings or amount in excess of $10. Massachusetts Laws Annot. 154 § 2.
Michigan	$3,500, not to exceed 40 acres if rural or one lot in city. Michigan Stat Annot. 27A.6023.	100% of earnings.
Minnesota	160 acres if outside city; 1/2 acre if in city. Minnesota Stat. 510.01.	Lesser of excess of 40 times federal minimum wage or 25% of earnings. Minnesota Stat. 571.55.
Mississippi	160 acres not to exceed $30,000 in value. Mississippi Cons. Annot. 85-3-21.	0% for 30 days then lesser of excess of 30 times federal minimum wage or 25% of earnings. Mississippi Cons. Annot. 85-3-4.
Missouri	None.	Lesser of excess of 30 times federal minimum wage or 25% of earnings. (10% if head of house.) Missouri Stat. 525.030.
Montana	$40,000, including traceable proceeds for 18 months. Montana Cons. Annot. 70-32-104.	Lesser of excess of 30 times federal minimum wage or 25% of earnings. Montana Cons. Annot. 25-13-614.

Figure 6.1 State Homestead and Income Exemptions (Continued)

Nebraska	160 acres if outside city;1/2 acre in city, not to exceed $10,000 in value. Nebraska Stat. 1943 § 40-101.	Lesser of excess of 30 times federal minimum wage or 25% of earnings. (15% if head of house.) Nebraska Stat. 1943 § 25-1558.
Nevada	$95,000; must declare in writing. Nevada Stat 115.01.	Lesser of excess of 30 times federal minimum wage or 25% of earnings. Nevada Stat. 21.090.
New Hampshire	$5,000. New Hampshire Rev. Stat. Annot. § 480:1.	100% of earnings.
New Jersey	None.	100% over $7,500 per year; 10% if more than $48 per week and $7,500 for year; 0% if earnings are less than $48 per week. New Jersey Stat. Annot. 2A:17-50.
New Mexico	$20,000. New Mexico Stat. 42-10-9.	Lesser of excess of 40 times federal minimum wage or 25% of earnings. New Mexico Stat. 35-12-7.
New York	$10,000. New York Civ. Prac. Law 5206	100% of earnings.
North Carolina	$7,500, offset by personal claims. North Carolina Stat. 1C-1601.	60 days of earnings. North Carolina Stat. 1-362.
North Dakota	$80,000, including proceeds from sale. North Dakota Cons. 47-18-1.	Lesser of excess of 40 times federal minimum wage or 25% of earnings. North Dakota Cons. 28-22-2.
Ohio	$5,000, offset by personal claim. Ohio Rev. Code 2329.66	Lesser of excess of 30 times federal minimum wage or 25% of earnings. Ohio Rev. Code 2329.66.

Figure 6.1   State Homestead and Income Exemptions (Continued)

Oklahoma	160 acres if outside city; 1 acre if inside city; not to exceed $5,000 in value. Oklahoma Stat. Annot. 1A1.	25% of earnings. Oklahoma Stat. Annot. 1A18.
Oregon	60 acres outside city; 1 block in city, not to exceed $15,000 in value. Oregon Rev. Stat. 23.240.	Lesser of excess of 40 times federal minimum wage or 25% of earnings. Oregon Rev. Stat. 23.185.
Pennsylvania	None.	0% of earnings. Pennsylvania Cons. Stat. 8127.
Rhode Island	None.	Earnings in excess of $50 per week. Rhode Island Laws 9-26-4.
South Carolina	$5,000, offset by personal claims. South Carolina Cons. Stat. 15-41-30.	0% of earnings. South Carolina Cons. Stat. 15-39-410.
South Dakota	100% protected South Dakota Cons. Laws 43-31-1.	0% for 60 days. South Dakota Cons. Laws 15-20-12.
Tennessee	$5,000 ($7,500 jointly). Tennessee Cons. Annot. 26-2-30.	Lesser of excess of 30 times federal minimum wage or 25% of earnings. Tennessee Cons. Annot. 26-2-106.
Texas	100 acres (200 for family) outside city; 1 acre in city. Texas Prop. Code 41.001.	0% of earnings. Texas Annot Rev. Stat. 4099.
Utah	$8,000 for head of house, includes traceable proceeds for one year. Utah Cons. Annot. 78-23-3.	100% of earnings.
Vermont	$30,000. Vermont Stat. Annot. 101.	Lesser of excess of 30 times federal minimum wage or 25% of earnings. Vermont Stat. Annot. 3170.

Figure 6.1   State Homestead and Income Exemptions (Continued)

Virginia	$5,000 offset by personal exemption claim. Virginia Stat. 34-4.	Lesser of excess of 30 times federal minimum wage or 25% of earnings. Virginia Stat. 34-29.
Washington	$30,000, including traceable proceeds for one year. Washington Stat. 6.12.010.	Lesser of excess of 30 times federal minimum wage or 25% of earnings. Washington Stat. 7.33.280.
West Virginia	$5,000 for head of house. West Virginia Cons. 38-9-1.	100% of earnings.
Wisconsin	$40,000, including traceable proceeds for 2 years if intent to purchase new homestead. Wisconsin Stat. Annot. 815.21.	Lesser of excess of 30 times federal minimum wage or 25% of earnings. Wisconsin Stat. Annot. 815.18
Wyoming	$10,000; must be owner occupied. ·Wyoming Stat. Annot. 1-20-101.	50% of earnings. Wyoming Stat. Annot. 1-17-411.
District of Columbia	None.	Lesser of excess of 30 times federal minimum wage or 25% of earnings. District of Columbia Civ. 16-572.

7

Using Trusts and Joint Tenancies To Protect Your Assets

The form under which property is owned plays a vital role in any asset protection program. Essentially, you may hold property in your own name (or jointly with another person) or you may choose to put the property into a trust. Depending upon how you structure the ownership, both individual ownership and trusts can protect many of your personal assets.

Trusts

There are two primary purposes for creating a trust:

1. Tax planning and savings for estates, and

2. Maintaining privacy with respect to your personal finances and transactions.

Both of these requirements can be satisfied by a trust. A properly written spendthrift trust bars creditors from reaching the assets placed in it. The spendthrift trust, therefore, protects the property against the claims of two sets of creditors—those of the person who establishes the trust as well as those of the trust's beneficiary.

In addition to asset protection, a trust provides a family with the ability to:

• transfer wealth from parent to child;

- reduce the costs of probate, and

- provide an independent trustee to manage the finances of individuals who may not be able to take care of themselves.

It is beyond the scope of this book to examine the tax advantages of trusts, but before creating a trust you must look into the tax concerns.

In essence, there are two types of trusts: *revocable* and *irrevocable*. The level of asset protection depends on the type of trust chosen, the powers you retain and the term or life of the trust. Trusts can be established during your life or by your will.

Irrevocable Trust

The term irrevocable means that once established you no longer have the right or authority to change or alter the terms of the trust. There is one exception to this rule: most state laws will allow you to nominate successor trustees without breaking the irrevocability of the trust.

The irrevocable trust is the most potent trust vehicle for asset protection. The strength of this strategy stems from the fact that you have completely and irrevocably transferred ownership of the property to another. In effect, you have gifted the property away. The property is shielded from your creditors because you no longer own it, and you will not be getting the property back in the future. As always, you must be careful that the transfer to the trust is not considered a fraudulent conveyance. If so, your creditors may be able to break the protections of the trust.

You cannot be both the grantor (the person setting up the trust) and the beneficiary (the person who receives income and/or the principal of the trust). Most states do not recognize *spendthrift trusts* if the person who sets up the trust and the beneficiary are the same individual. This is considered a fraudulent transfer on its face.

How do you set up an irrevocable trust? To accomplish asset protection, it is critically important that the trust be carefully written and that all irrevocable trust criteria are satisfied completely. The most important decision you will make is identifying the trustee. You should not be the trustee. You do not want to give even the least impression that you are still the owner of the property, and under trust law the trustee is the *legal title owner* of the property in the trust.

Who is to be the beneficiary? The beneficiary is the person who ultimately receives or benefits from the property. It can be anyone, but most likely the beneficiary of your irrevocable trust will be your spouse or children, or, if you are not married, another family membes. What the trust accomplishes is to delay the outright transfer of the trust property to the beneficiary until some established future time or event. The trust document defines that future time or event. The time can be measured in years, e.g., ten years from the establishment of the trust. An event can be a predetermined occurrence, such as someone retiring from work or dying.

The Irrevocable Minor's Trust

The Tax Reform Act of 1986 gutted the tax benefits that had been available from Minor's Trusts. The ability to *split income* between a parent and child, taking advantage of the child's lower income bracket, has been removed for children under age 14. However, in the asset protection realm the Minor's Trust is still a valuable tool.

A Minor's Trust is a vehicle that enables parents to make gifts of property to their children and ensure that the property is protected until the child is mature enough not to waste the gift. Further, the use of the trust places the property in the hands of a trustee, thereby allowing the property to be disposed of properly even while the child is a minor. Remember, a minor is allowed to disavow any contracts they entered into prior to their reaching the age of majority.

The Minor's Trust is governed by two subsections of the Internal Revenue Code—Section 2503(b) and (c). Both subsections set the age of majority at 21, regardless of your state's law. The benefit of a Minor's Trust is that your creditors cannot reach the assets transferred into the trust, nor can your child's creditors reach the assets while they are in the trust.

Section 2503(c) Minor's Trusts

A 2503(c) Minor's Trust requires the trust to distribute any retained principal and income that has not been paid for the benefit of the beneficiary on his or her 21st birthday. Further, it requires that should the minor die prior to reaching age 21, his or her interest must be paid to the child's estate.

The law allows a 2503(c) Minor's Trust to continue past the individual's 21st birthday, but only if no restrictions bar the beneficiary from getting the trust property at any point in time after turning 21.

This trust blocks creditors from reaching property that you intend to use to take care of your children. During your child's minority, it can also protect property from your children's creditors. The trust cannot, however, stop your children's creditors from reaching the property after your children turn 21.

Section 2503(b) Minor's Trusts

A better alternative might be the 2503(b) Minor's Trust. In a sense the term *Minor's Trust* is a misnomer, because the trust can last beyond a person's minority. It can last even as long as the beneficiary's entire life. Another difference between the 2503(b) and (c) Minor's Trusts is that the 2503(b) Minor's Trust must distribute the income it earns at least once a year. However, the principal of the trust does not have to be distributed to the income beneficiary. That is, you can have income payable to your child for life, and upon the child's death, the principal can be paid to his or her children.

The Section 2503(b) trust provides limited protection from creditors. Creditors cannot reach the principal of the trust, but the income—if distributed directly to your child—may be attached by their creditors.

Both forms of Minor's Trust can have income tax ramifications for both you and your child. If your children are under age 14, the income that is distributed to them for their benefit will be taxed at your personal rate. Any income that is retained in the 2503(c) trust will be taxed at trust tax rates, which are generally higher than individual tax rates. Finally, if the trust is used to pay for support obligations, the parents might have income, since they would be relieved from a support obligation.

_____

This is also an issue of state law. Do you have an obligation to pay for the education of your child? This is an emerging issue in many states. For tax purposes, the only reported case is from New Jersey where the tax court determined that under local law, the parents were required to pay for the college cost of their child. Therefore, the trust paying for the college expense relieved the parents of their parental obligation and resulted in taxable income to the parents.

Life Insurance Trusts

Life insurance, in today's market, is more than *just insurance*—it is an asset. Many insurance policies are designed to provide income or an investment that will grow tax-free. As such, insurance is an asset that may be attacked by your creditors.

Keep in mind that, in the business loan setting, most lenders will require the assignment of insurance as additional collateral for loans. If your insurance is to be used to provide for the care of your family, it is imperative that you plan to insulate the insurance from your creditors.

The procedure used to establish a life insurance trust is similar to that used to establish trusts generally. This procedure requires a written document, a trustee, a beneficiary and terms of distribution. Life insurance trusts generally are established with more concern for tax savings than asset protection. However, as noted, some insurance policies can accumulate significant value other than as a death benefit.

The life insurance trust can be revocable or irrevocable. The irrevocable insurance trust provides the greatest asset protection. The trust can be *unfunded*, meaning that the only asset the trust owns is the insurance policy on your life. Such a trust is considered unfunded because the insurance contract is a promise to pay later and, for that reason, does not become a tangible asset until the insured's death.

Insurance can also be placed in a revocable or living trust. As an asset protection strategy, this provides little protection. As will be discussed, the grantor (the individual who establishes the trust) is treated as the owner of property in a revocable trust since that individual has the ability, by the terms of the trust, to terminate the trust at any time. The revocable insurance trust is more properly an estate tax device than an asset protection tool.

Revocable Trusts

Revocable trusts get their name from their nature. You can revoke such a trust at any time during your life. A revocable trust becomes irrevocable at your death since you are the only person who can alter, amend or terminate the trust. Upon your death, since no one has the power to subsequently change the trust—at least without court approval—the trust becomes irrevocable.

Revocable trusts offer no asset protection if the trust is for your benefit during your life. The general rule is that a person cannot be his or her own trustee and, therefore, the trust's assets are reachable by creditors.

What if you have an independent trustee? In that situation, state laws vary. You may successfully exempt some property from creditors by virtue of your not having ownership over the property.

As with many of the techniques we've discussed, a revocable trust does not grant immunity, but it may dissuade a less than enthusiastic creditor from pursuing your property. If your debt is not sufficient to justify the legal expenses involed, your creditor may not be willing to sue to reduce his or her claim to judgment, and force you to revoke your revocable trust and turn over the proceeds.

The strongest protection offered by a revocable trust comes into existence when the grantor dies. At that point, the trust becomes irrevocable, and the beneficiaries will receive the property according to the terms of the trust.

When the grantor dies, the grantor's creditors may be out of luck. If funded prior to the grantor's death, the revocable trust need not pay creditors out of the trust estate unless there has been a fraudulent transfer.

The Foreign-Based Trust

The foreign-based trust is perhaps the newest asset protection program to have been developed. It is easily the safest form of asset protection available today. Designed primarily for professionals who fear outlandish judgments in malpractice litigation and business people who are concerned with extensive liability flowing from deals that go bad, the foreign-based trust overcomes all of the drawbacks of every other trust form.

The benefits of the foreign-based trust are remarkable. First, such a trust protects the principal from attacks by creditors, even in situations that could be termed fraudulent under U.S. law. Second, it allows the grantor to receive income from the trust and to maintain effective control over the ways in which the trust's principal is invested and distributed.

The foreign-based trust is established in much the same way any other trust is created. Under the terms of a written trust agreement, a grantor places assets in a trust, names a trustee and identifies the beneficiary. The only difference between this form of trust and others we have discussed is that it is created under the laws of a friendly foreign jurisdiction, such as the Isle of Mann or the Cook Islands. Should you be concerned that creating a trust in a foreign jurisdiction is a risky venture, you should be advised that the Isle of Mann is a British protectorate located several miles off the shores of Scotland and that the Cook Islands are a dependency of New Zealand. Both are stable, secure jurisdictions, and both have very favorable trust laws.

By setting up your foreign-based trust in a friendly jurisdiction, you will be gaining the advantages of laws that permit you to create an irrevocable trust in which you are the named beneficiary. Although you will have to name an independent trustee who is a resident of the foreign jurisdiction, you can replace the trustee at any time if he or she does not satisfy your standards. Further, the trust document can require the trustee to get your approval before making an investment or a distribution of assets. You, therefore, remain in control.

For the most part, these foreign jurisdictions prohibit creditors from reaching assets placed in an irrevocable trust. They set up roadblocks to stop creditors who seek to pierce a trust on the grounds that the trust was created in a fraudulent manner. Such foreign jurisdictions will not recognize a judgment from a court in this country to the effect that the grantor acted fraudulently. Instead, if the creditor wishes to make that claim, he or she must do so in the courts of the foreign jurisdiction and must prove its case under the laws of that jurisdiction.

For example, if a creditor wishes to enforce a judgment against you, he or she must go to the Cook Islands (about 1,800 miles northeast of New Zealand), sue you all over again, and prove the case against you all over again (but, this time under Cook Islands law). Equally important, the Cook Islands law takes a much different approach to defining a fraudulent transfer than do the laws of the states of this country. Obviously, they are more favorable to the debtor.

Foreign-based trusts are not for everyone. First, they cannot be created on a do-it-yourself basis. You will need the assistance of a qualified lawyer, and the fees for such services run as high as $15,000. The annual fee for the trustee may range from $1,000 to $2,500 a year. Given those costs, the foreign-based trust probably is the tool of choice for individuals who are exposed to the risks of massive judgments. For those people, however, the foreign-based trust is—beyond any doubt—a virtually impregnable shield for asset protection purposes.

The Medicaid Trust

The Medicaid Trust was created to protect individuals from the cost of a catastrophic illness. It is a form of irrevocable trust that may have only limited value against business or personal creditors, but it is an invaluable tool should the person creating the trust fall victim to a catastrophic illness.

A jointly financed federal-state program established to provide medical treatment for the poor and indigent, Medicaid offers comprehensive coverage that includes prescription drugs, hospital treatment, physician care and other medical services.

The Medicaid Trust ensures that the principal amount you place in the trust cannot be used by the state to disqualify you from Medicaid assistance. Medicaid assistance is limited to individuals who, for our purposes, have virtually no meaningful assets to their name.

Generally an individual cannot have countable assets in excess of $2,000 to $3,000. Noncountable assets or exempt assets include: your primary residence, household furnishings, one wedding ring, one automobile, prepaid funeral expenses and court-ordered support payments. The amount or value of the property, which is either exempt or may be owned, is determined by each state. Check your state Medicaid office for the limits set by your state's laws.

A Medicaid Trust is formed in much the same way as other trusts—the grantor places assets in an irrevocable trust and names another person as the trustee. Unlike other types of irrevocable trusts, however, the grantor is named as the income beneficiary and either a spouse or children as the beneficiaries of the trust's principal.

That means that the grantor will continue to enjoy the income of the trust's assets for the rest of his or her life. In the event the grantor should require extended or permanent nursing care, he or she will qualify for Medicaid and will have the funds to supplement Medicaid assistance in order to choose an appropriate nursing facility.

Because the income from the trust goes back to the grantor, creditors of the grantor can reach that money to satisfy their claims, and, in many states, may be able to reach the principal amount put into the trust.

The Medicaid Trust is a special purpose trust. It is not designed to protect your assets from creditor attack. Instead, it is used to ensure that should a crippling illness arise, the principal that you worked a lifetime to create will not be lost to hospitals and nursing care centers. This trust enables you to qualify for Medicaid, and, if necessary, to procure assistance at a higher level than Medicaid will provide.

There are two practical matters you should keep in mind if you believe you probably do not need a Medicaid Trust. First, current research indicates that seven out of every ten people will be forced to consider the need for long-term medical care during their lifetime and that the cost of such care in a nursing home ranges between $25,000 and $50,000 a year. Second, you cannot expect to gain the benefits of a Medicaid Trust if you wait until disaster strikes. The general rule for Medicaid is that eligibility for benefits will be denied to an individual who has transferred nonexempt assets within 30 months of being institutionalized. As a result, you must retain enough assets to pay for at least 30 months of private pay as the patient or transfer your property 30 months before being institutionalized.

The significance of the Medicaid Trust becomes clear when you consider the situation of the person whose planning does not anticipate the possibility of a catastrophic illness. If the illness lingers, most, if not all of the person's life savings will go to nursing home care. A Medicaid Trust protects the principal invested in it from the state and the nursing home. Since that principal is not a countable asset, it will not prevent you from obtaining Medicaid assistance. By combining that assistance with the income from the Medicaid Trust, you can select the nursing home of your choice as opposed to a state-operated facility.

Business Trusts

Business trusts are more typically known as *Massachusetts Business Trusts (MBT)*, since Massachusetts was the first state to recognize them. In essence, an MBT provides for the operation of property or a business in a trust format. The MBT grants the trust certificate holders limited liability, much like what a corporation is permitted to offer its shareholders. Many states, however, require some form of registration of the MBT. For federal tax purposes, an MBT is treated as a corporation. For these reasons, it may be just as easy and efficient to form a corporation as it is to start an MBT.

The primary advantage of an MBT over a corporation is that the affairs of the MBT are private. But in any contested litigation, the privacy of the MBT does not become a privilege limiting a creditor's right to obtain information.

Many states require strict adherence to their statutes to obtain the limited liability benefit of an MBT. Failure to do so might result in your having personal liability for business obligations.

All things considered, the corporate form of a business is a safer vehicle for providing protection from business debts than an MBT.

Land Trusts

Some trust strategies provide only a false sense of security as an asset protector. This is particularly true in the case of a land trust. Created under state law, the land trust is a special form of revocable trust.

The primary benefit of a land trust is the privacy it provides for the trust owners. When a property is titled in the name of the land trust, creditors searching the recorder of deeds will only find the name of the trustee, not the true owners. This provides *protection* from reverse research, that is, finding the owner based on the property. It does not protect you from disclosing your interest if you are directly asked by a creditor, particularly if the inquiry comes when you are under oath.

As with many strategies adopted to protect assets from creditors, the more complicated the strategy the more complications that will arise regarding the disposition of assets. Although a trustee will not disclose to outsiders who the owners of the property are, the trustee may not want to accept liability for some transactions. The trustee may require you to dissolve the trust in order to sell the property.

In addition, a major drawback to a land trust is that your ownership in the trust is not considered ownership of the land for federal tax purposes. Instead you are deemed to own personal property, not real property. This will impact your ability to claim a homestead exemption (see Chapter 6) and your ability to transfer the land in a like-kind exchange under Internal Revenue Code Section 1031. Further, dissolving the trust just to enter into a like-kind exchange may not result in the property qualifying for the tax-free treatment.

Finally, the land trust may result in additional costs to you. Some states will require the payment of transfer taxes on each transfer in and out of the trust to the beneficial owners. Check with your state's recorder of deeds office to find out if you must pay a transfer tax.

Bolstering the Asset Protection of a Trust

- *If possible, use an irrevocable trust.* As discussed, you give away the property in an irrevocable trust so that neither your creditors nor your beneficiaries' creditors, can reach the property while the assets are held in trust.
- *Have a nonprotection reason for establishing the trust.* This is similar to having a *business purpose* for pursuing some transactions. Courts are loathe to pierce trusts as asset protectors if the trust has been established for estate planning purposes or to provide for the education of a family member.
- *Choose an independent trustee.* You should not be the trustee. An outsider, no matter how friendly, must exercise his or her own fiduciary duty to the trust. If the trust limits or establishes objective guidelines on how the trustee can invest trust property, the courts generally do not look beyond the terms of the trust.

Joint Ownership

The most common form of property ownership in the family situation is *joint ownership*, since it eases the eventual disposition of property. It allows more than one person to have access to and benefit from the property. For example, consider how many people have joint checking or savings accounts. This type of ownership is not limited to married people. To the contrary, many joint accounts are between parents and children, especially for elderly parents who may need the help of children in their daily financial affairs.

In this section we will briefly examine the different types of joint ownership and the difficulties they create for the judgment creditor.

Types of Co-Ownership

There are three types of co-ownership—*tenants in common, joint tenants* and *tenants by the entirety.* Each co-tenancy creates specific legal rights, and state law determines how a creditor can attack the property when held in a joint title.

Tenants in Common

A tenants in common form of ownership creates an interest in the property that is divided among the co-owners. This ownership allows each individual to sell or transfer his or her interest in the property without the consent of the other tenants.

This transferability feature exposes a tenant in common's interest in property to execution by his or her creditors. The creditor can either take the debtor's interest, request that the court sell the property or, in the case of securities or land, partition the property and then sell it.

Joint Tenancy

The primary difference between joint tenancy and tenants in common is the fact that a joint tenancy creates an undivided interest in property. The joint tenancy can be either equal or unequal ownership interests, depending upon the titling.

Joint tenancy generally must be established by a written document. In the case of real estate, the deed satisfies the need for a writing if it transfers the property to two or more individuals as joint tenants. Most states require some recitation that a joint tenancy has been created or they will treat the co-ownership as a tenants in common relationship.

The strength of joint tenancy in protecting assets lies in the fact that each tenant has an undivided interest. This undivided nature of ownership dissuades creditors in two ways—the value of an undivided interest is less than that of a divided interest, and the ability to cause a partition of the property is greatly reduced.

Many states no longer presume that a joint tenancy creates a right of survivorship. Therefore, the titling of the property should reflect that the right of survivorship exists. With a right of survivorship, joint tenancy is similar to a winner-take-all pool. During the lives of the tenants, they can all agree to sell or end this form of ownership, but the last tenant to survive inherits all.

There are some limitations affecting joint tenancy:

- It only covers property that is actually titled as joint tenants.

- It provides flexibility to both joint tenants, but creates no obligation for the joint tenant to use the property for your benefit.

- The joint tenants may use the property for their own purposes, i.e. to pay off their own debts.

- A joint tenancy with right of survivorship may unintentionally disinherit other heirs, while giving the joint tenant a windfall.

Tenants by the Entirety

Tenants by the entirety is a special form of joint tenants that may be established only by husbands and wives. The ownership of property in tenants by the entirety may only be transferred on the agreement of both husband and wife, and the survivor inherits the property on the death of the other. Of special importance is that tenants by the entirety property does not pass according to a will; it passes by operation of law to the survivor.

The benefit of this form of ownership is that creditors cannot attach and sell the property unless both owners are party to the debt. Accordingly, if one person has a large judgment or debt against himself or herself, the creditor cannot get the property if the other spouse is not a party to the debt. One caution: if the non-debtor spouse dies, the creditor can perfect his or her claim and take the property. Conversely, if the debtor dies first, the creditor cannot reach the property.

Let's look at a recent case to see how strong an asset protector the tenants by entirety doctrine is. In Pennsylvania, a husband borrowed money from a bank. His wife did not cosign the loan, but she did consent to guarantee the loan. When the man defaulted on the loan, the bank obtained judgment against him on the loan and against his wife on the guarantee. The Pennsylvania Supreme Court refused to allow the bank to satisfy the judgment against the couple's joint tenant property. The court reasoned that only when the creditor obtains judgment against both tenants by entireties—when both are primary debtors or both are guarantors—can the creditor execute against the joint tenancy property.

Several states have abolished the tenancy by the entirety concept, but about half of the states still recognize it. In some states, e.g., Pennsylvania, tenants by the entirety completely bars creditors from executing against joint property for individual debts.

Figure 7.1 Establishing an Irrevocable Trust

TRUST AGREEMENT made the   day of   , 19   , by and between

(hereinafter referred to as the "Settlors") and

(hereinafter referred to as the "Trustee").

1. **Property of Settlors.** The Settlors transfer, assign, convey and quitclaim to the Trustee and to its successors in trust, the property described in Schedule "A", attached hereto, to have and to hold such property and any other property of any kind which the Trustee may, at any time, hereafter hold or acquire pursuant to any of the provisions hereof (all of which property is referred to hereinafter as the "Trust Estate"), subject to the trust, purposes, and conditions set forth.

2. **Additional Property.** Either of the Settlors or any other person shall have the right at any time, to transfer, assign and convey, deliver, devise and bequeath to the Trustee any additional cash, security, and other property in addition to the property presently transferred and delivered, or by having the proceeds of insurance policies made payable to the Trustee or by bequest or devise by will having proceeds payable to the Trustee and such cash, security, life insurance proceeds, and other property shall be held, administered, and disposed of by the Trustee as part of the trust estate in accordance with the provisions of this Trust Agreement without the execution of any further instrument or declaration.

3. **Insurance Policies.** The Settlors have caused or may cause the Trustee to be named as beneficiary of the insurance policies listed in the Schedule "B", attached hereto, and the Trustee accepts the designation in trust for the purposes and on the conditions set forth. The Settlors or any other person may at any time add any additional policy or policies of insurance to this Trust by assigning the policy or policies to the Trustee or by naming the Trustee as beneficiary. In either case, the policy and its proceeds shall be subject to the terms and conditions of this Agreement.

4. **Trustee's Duties During the Lifetime of the Settlors.** During the lifetime of the Settlors, the Trustee shall hold the Trust Fund for the following purposes:
   (a) The Trustee shall collect the income of the trust property and may in his discretion, apply the net income to the payment of premiums on any life insurance policy owned by the trust. If the net income is insufficient to pay such premiums, the Trustee may notify in writing the Settlors and the beneficiaries of the trust of such insufficiency and give them the opportunity to furnish the necessary funds. If neither the Settlors nor any of the beneficiaries furnish the funds necessary to pay the premiums, the Trustee may, but is not required to obtain the funds required to pay such premiums by selling a portion of the trust principal, or borrowing on the security of the trust principal, by borrowing against

Figure 7.1   Establishing an Irrevocable Trust (Continued)

the cash surrender value of the policy to pay premiums on other policies. The Trustee is also authorized to convert such policy to paid up or extended term insurance if the Trust Fund does not have the necessary funds to pay the premiums. If no funds are available for the payment of premiums on the policy, the Trustee is authorized to distribute such policy to the beneficiaries of the Trust named hereunder living at the time of the distribution.

(b) If there is any trust income remaining after the payment of premiums in accordance with (a) above, such income shall be added to the principal of the Trust.

(c) During the lifetime of either of the Settlors, any direct, indirect or deemed transfer to the Trust, whether in cash or other property, shall be subject to withdrawal pro rata under the provisions of this article by the beneficiaries of this Trust (herein this paragraph and in paragraph (d) following referred to as the "Donees"). Each pro rated right of withdrawal shall not exceed an amount for each Donee of the greater of Twenty Thousand Dollars ($20,000) or the amount of the gift tax annual exclusion under Section 2503(b) and 2513 of the Internal Revenue Code of 1986, as amended from time to time. The Trustee shall notify the Donees, in writing, of its receipt of any property over which their power of withdrawal can be exercised. Within thirty (30) days after their receipt of such notice, the Donees may exercise their power of withdrawal by informing the Trustee, in writing, of the amount they are withdrawing. If the Donees do not exercise their power of withdrawal within such thirty (30) day period, their power shall lapse with respect to the property covered by the notification. The Trustee is directed to hold a sufficient amount of the trust property in cash or in a form readily convertible to cash so that it may satisfy any exercise by the donees of their power of withdrawal. The Trustee may satisfy the exercise of any withdrawal right by distributing to the donee cash or other property, including life insurance policies. If any of the Donees is a minor or is otherwise under a disability, such as incompetency, guardian, committee, conservator or other authorized representative of the Donees may exercise the power of withdrawal on that Donee's behalf provided that under no circumstances may either of the Settlors so act on behalf of the Donees. If any Donee files for bankruptcy, that Donee's power of withdrawal shall be forfeited.

(d) Notwithstanding any of the provisions above, if, upon the termination or lapse of any power of withdrawal, the Donee holding the power would be deemed to have made a taxable gift for federal gift tax purposes, such power shall continue in existence with respect to the amount that would have been a taxable gift, except to the extent it shall thereafter terminate as provided in this paragraph. Such power shall terminate as soon as and to the extent that termination shall not result in a taxable gift by the Donee holding the power.

Figure 7.1 Establishing an Irrevocable Trust (Continued)

5. **Trustee's Duties Upon the Death of Either or Both Settlors.** Upon the death of either or both of the Settlors, the Trustee shall receive such sums of money as shall be due it under the terms of the policies of life insurance, including double indemnity benefits, and hold them in trust for the uses set forth. To facilitate the receipt of these sums of money, the Trustee shall have the power to execute and deliver receipts and other instruments, to compromise or adjust disputed claims in the manner as is in it's sole discretion, to use any funds in its hands, whether principal or income, to pay the costs and expenses, including attorney's fees, of bringing an action for the collection of the proceeds of any policy, and may reimburse itself for any advances made for such purposes. Upon payment to the Trustee of the amounts due under the policies of insurance, the insurance companies issuing these policies shall be relieved of all further liability and no company shall be under any responsibility to see to the performance of the trust.

6. **Dispositive Provisions.**
   (a) *Lifetime Trust.* During the lifetime of the Settlors, the Trustee shall hold all of the Trust Estate for the benefit of the children of the Settlor, (hereinafter referred to collectively as the "Beneficiaries" or individually as a "Beneficiary"). The Trustee shall, so long as at least one of the Settlors is alive, maintain the principal and accumulate all income within the Trust.
   (b) *Death of Both of the Settlors.* Upon the death of both of the Settlors, the Trustees shall divide the Trust Estate, as then constituted, into equal shares per stirpes so that there will be one share for each of the Beneficiaries named above. The income and principal of each of such shares shall be held and disposed of as hereinafter provided:
      (i) The income from each share so provided for each Beneficiary shall be paid in convenient installments to such Beneficiary. In addition to income, the Trustee shall be fully authorized to pay or expend and apply for the benefit of such Beneficiary such sums from the principal of his or her share as the Trustee considers necessary or desirable from time to time for his or her medical care, maintenance, education (including college education, both graduate and undergraduate), and support, taking into consideration all other income available to such beneficiary for such purposes from all sources known to the Trustee.
      (ii) When a Beneficiary reaches the age of forty (40) years, or upon division of the Trust into shares if such Beneficiary has then reached such age, the Trustee shall distribute to such Beneficiary one-third (1/3) in value of the principal of his or her share, then held hereunder; when a Beneficiary reaches the age of forty-five (45) years, or upon division of the Trust into shares if such child has then reached such age, the Trustee shall distribute to such Beneficiary one-half (1/2) in value of the principal of his or her

Figure 7.1 Establishing an Irrevocable Trust (Continued)

share, then held hereunder; and when a Beneficiary reaches the age of fifty (50) years, or upon division of the Trust into shares, if such child has then reached such age, the Trustee shall distribute to such Beneficiary the balance of his or her share.

(iii) In the event of the death of a Beneficiary prior to complete distribution of his or her share, or at the time such share is created, if such Beneficiary is then dead, then upon such Beneficiary's death or upon the setting up of such Beneficiary's share or the remainder thereof, the aforesaid shall be distributed per stirpes to his or her then living issue, if any, or if none then per stirpes to the then living issue of the Settlors, the share of any Beneficiary whose original share is then being held in trust to be added to and treated as part of that trust. If no child of the Settlors, nor the issue of any deceased child of the Settlors is living, then the proceeds of the Trust Estate shall be distributed to the heirs at law of.

7. **Income Accumulation.** The Trustees shall accumulate income in whole or in part, if in it's discretion such income is not required for the purposes of this Trust in a particular year. Accumulated income shall be added to principal and may be expended in the same manner as principal.

8. **Irrevocability.** The Settlors hereby declare that this Trust Agreement is irrevocable, and cannot be altered, amended, or revoked at any time.

9. **Powers of Trustee.** The proceeds of the insurance policies, together with all other property held or which may be acquired by the Trustee hereunder, shall constitute the Trust Estate. In addition to the powers conferred by the common law, by statute, or by other provisions hereof, the Trustee is hereby empowered:

    (a) to hold, possess, manage and control the Trust Estate for the purposes herein set forth;

    (b) to invest and reinvest all or any part of the Trust Estate in such stocks, bonds, mutual funds, common trust funds, securities or other property, real or personal, including stock or other securities of any corporate fiduciary or of a holding company controlling said fiduciary, as in the Trustee's discretion Trustee shall deem proper, without regard to statutes limiting the property which Trustee may purchase;

    (c) to sell, transfer, exchange, or otherwise dispose of, any part of the Trust Estate, for cash or on terms, at public or private sale, and to pledge or encumber the same;

    (d) to lease any real estate held hereunder for any term, notwithstanding the duration of the Trust;

    (e) to execute and deliver any deeds, leases, assignment or other instruments as may be necessary to carry out the provisions of this Trust;

    (f) to open and maintain in the name of the Trust, bank accounts, safe deposit boxes and other adequate measures for the safeguarding of property;

Figure 7.1 Establishing an Irrevocable Trust (Continued)

(g) to exercise any subscription right in connection with any security held hereunder, and to consent to or participate in any reorganization, consolidation, or merger of any corporation;

(h) to make any distribution hereunder either in kind or in money. Distributions in kind shall be made at the market value of the property distributed and the Trustee may, in Trustee's discretion, cause the share to be transferred to any distributee to be composed of property like or different from that transferred to any other distributee;

(i) to conduct any business which may become a part of the Trust Estate for such period as the Trustees may deem proper, with power to borrow money and pledge the assets of such business, and to delegate such powers to any partner, manager or employee, without liability for any loss occurring therein. The Trustee may make public or private sale of such business, and the real and personal property thereof, at such time or times, and for such price or prices, and upon such terms as to cash and credit, with or without security for the purchase price, as the Trustee may deem best;

. (j) The Trustee may, if the Trustee deems it wise, and without being required to obtain leave of court, organize a corporation to carry on such business, if unincorporated, by itself or jointly with others, and may contribute all or part of the property of such business as capital to such corporation and may accept stock in the corporation in lieu thereof. Similarly, the Trustee may dissolve any corporation carrying on any such business and may operate such business in any other form that the Trustee in Trustee's discretion, deems appropriate;

(k) to engage attorneys, accountants, agents, custodians, clerks, investment counsel and such other persons as the Trustee may deem advisable, and to make such payments therefore as the Trustee may deem reasonable, and to charge the expenses thereof to income or principal as the Trustee may determine, and to delegate to such persons any discretion which the Trustee may deem proper;

(l) to do all such acts, take all such proceedings and to exercise all rights and privileges, although not hereinbefore specifically mentioned, with relation to any such property, as if the absolute owners thereof, and in connection therewith to make, execute and deliver any instruments and to enter into any covenants or agreements binding any trust created hereunder;

(m) to purchase securities on margins and to rehypothecate same.

10. **Compensation of Trustees.** The Trustee shall be reimbursed out of the trust estate for any advances made by him and for all reasonable expenses incurred in the management and protection of the trust estate, and for the employment of any agents, attorneys, accountants, and investment analysts and the like engaged by it for the protection and administration of the trust estate.

Figure 7.1 Establishing an Irrevocable Trust (Continued)

11. **Bond and Liability of Trustee.** Neither the original Trustee nor any successor Trustee shall be required to give any bond or security for the faithful performance of their duties. However, if any bond is required by law, then the bond shall be in such minimum amount as to satisfy the requirements of the law. Any Trustee shall be liable only for his own willful breach of trust and for fraud and not for any honest error in judgment. In any agreement or contract made by the Trustees on behalf of the trust estate, such Trustee shall be authorized to stipulate and provide against personal liability on such contracts, and the rights and obligations created by virtue of such contract or contracts shall belong to the trust estate.

12. **Spendthrift Provision.** The beneficiaries shall have no right to anticipate, to pledge, to encumber or hypothecate or in any other manner to alienate his interest in either the income or the principal of the trust estate and his interest shall not be liable for his debts, contracts, or engagements or subject to execution, attachment, sequestration, or other legal process other than as specifically provided in accordance with these terms.

13. **Trustee's Account.** The Trustee shall keep a complete and permanent record of all receipts and investments and disbursements made for or on behalf of or on account of the trust estate. The Trustee shall render an account annually and shall make available for inspection the annual account to those beneficiaries who are entitled to apply for benefits in accordance with the terms of this Trust Agreement. Whenever requested to do so by any of the beneficiaries, the books of the Trustee shall be open to the inspection of the beneficiary at all reasonable times. Additionally, if this trust is funded during the life of the Settlors, then an annual account shall be sent to the Settlors by the Trustee.

14. **Succession and Resignation of Trustee.** The Trustee named in this Deed of Trust may resign without accounting or Court approval at any time by a written notice of resignation delivered to Settlors, if living, or if not, then to the successor Trustee which notice shall thereupon be attached to this Agreement. In the event of such resignation, a successor Trustee may be appointed by the Settlors during their lifetime, or, after both of their deaths, by any court having jurisdiction over the Trust. Any successor Trustee thus appointed shall succeed to all the duties and to all the powers, including discretionary powers, granted to the original Trustee.

15. **Termination of Trust.** Notwithstanding anything herein to the contrary, unless sooner terminated under other provisions hereto, all trusts herein created shall terminate twenty-one (21) years after the death of the last survivor of the Settlors, their children and grandchildren living at such time as this instrument becomes irrevocable and, upon such termination, the then Trustee shall distribute the remaining principal and income in the trust so terminated to the person or persons then entitled to receive the income therefrom in the proportions in which they are so entitled.

Figure 7.1   Establishing an Irrevocable Trust (Continued)

16. **Separability.** If any provisions of this Trust Agreement shall be held invalid or unenforceable, the remaining provisions shall continue to be fully effective.

17. **Law Governing Trusts.** All questions pertaining to the administration of this Trust or the construction or validity of this Trust shall be governed by the law of the State of

18. **Gender and Number.** Words importing the singular number and masculine gender herein, shall be understood to apply to one or more persons and to females as well as males.

IN WITNESS WHEREOF, the Settlors and the Trustee have set their hands and have caused this Trust Agreement to be executed on the day and year first above written.

WITNESS

_____

_____

Settlor

_____

Settlor

_____

Trustee

_____

8

Partnerships and Corporations

There are essentially three ways in which a business can be conducted:

1. The *sole proprietorship* in which an individual operates a business under his or her own name and assumes all of the liability for the debts of the business.

2. The *partnership* in which two or more persons form an association to carry on a business for profit as co-owners. Although the partnership entity is liable for the debts of the business, the partners themselves are jointly liable for all debts and liabilities. Partners, in a very real sense, bear the same potential liabilities as a sole proprietor. There is, however, a second form of partnership, known as the limited partnership, which has two categories of partners. One of those categories consists of limited partners whose liability for the debts of the business is restricted solely to the amount they invested to purchase their limited partnership interest. This form of limited partnership, as we shall see, can be an important part of an asset protection program.

3. The *corporation* is an invaluable asset protection tool. It shields all of its participants from liability for the debts of the business. Properly structured, a corporation can provide the maximum protection against liability to third persons while offering the most attractive tax benefits to the owners of the business.

Before analyzing each of these business forms, it is important that you recognize the various factors involved in choosing one of these tools. For example, the first questions you must ask yourself are:

- *Am I looking for a business form primarily to protect me against the claims arising out of the operations of my business or profession?* If so, you'll probably want to consider the corporation as your primary tool.

- *Am I looking for a business form as an asset protection tool?* The assumption here is that the business form will not actively operate a trade or profession, but will be used as a *safety deposit box* into which assets can be poured in order to protect them from attack.

- *Will the business form create profits subject to federal or state taxation?* If so, you will find that certain forms are more favorable than others. With these considerations in mind, let's take a look at the three categories of business forms.

General Partnerships and Sole Proprietorship

Neither the general partnership nor the sole proprietorship can serve a meaningful role in an asset protection program. In fact, each is the very antithesis of an asset protection tool. As noted earlier, the sole proprietor and the partner in a general partnership can be held liable for all of the debts of the business if the enterprise is unable to meet its obligations. This means that the personal—non-business—assets of the sole proprietor or partner can be attacked to satisfy the debts of the business. This potential liability exceeds ordinary business debts; it even includes liability imposed upon the business because of an employee's negligence. Assume, for example, that you operate a retail food shop and an employee carelessly stacks a soft drink display. The display topples over, severely injuring a passing shopper. That shopper's ten million dollar lawsuit will name the business, its proprietor or partners and the stock clerk as the defendants in the lawsuit. If your business (and the insurance it carries) is not enough to satisfy the claim, then the plaintiff will come after your personal assets.

The sole proprietorship and the general partnership do provide several *alleged* benefits as business forms. Unlike corporations or limited partnerships, sole proprietorships can be formed without special filings in the state in which they operate. However, the filings for a limited partnership or corporation are rather simple, straightforward and relatively inexpensive. As we'll explain a bit later in this chapter, you can form your own corporation simply and inexpensively.

The other key advantage to the sole proprietorship is that it permits the business owner to avoid the double taxation that can be imposed on a corporation's profits. Again, this advantage is illusory since a corporation can be formed so that it enjoys partnership-like tax treatment, and a limited partnership, by definition, enjoys the single tax treatment of partnerships.

It is clear, therefore, that neither the sole proprietorship nor the general partnership offers any advantages for the individual who is concerned with shielding assets. Not only do these two business modes fail to protect any assets that may be placed in their care, but they can generate added exposure with respect to business obligations they create.

Understanding the Limited Partnership

A limited partnership is a business form that utilizes the best features of the corporation and the partnership. It receives the same favorable tax treatment that partnerships are accorded, and it provides the benefits of limited liability for its passive investors. The limited partnership is a business that consists of at least one general partner who manages the business and at least one limited partner who, as a passive investor, has no active voice in the management of the business and who cannot be held liable for the business's debts.

The general partner in a limited partnership is much like the partner in an ordinary partnership. The general partner can be held personally liable for the debts of the business. But, the general partner need not be a natural person, i.e., a human being. A corporation can be a general partner, and it will be liable for the debts of the limited partnership to the extent that it has assets.

The limited partners more closely resemble shareholders in a corporation than they do partners in a general partnership. A limited partner has no liability to third persons who have claims against the business. In fact, the total exposure of the limited partner is the investment he or she may have made in the business.

Because it offers the benefit of limited liability for its limited partners, a limited partnership can be created only if a state statute authorizes its existence. Except for Louisiana, every state authorizes the creation of limited partnerships. Most states have adopted a law based on the Uniform Limited Partnership Act; the few that have not adopted that act follow the revised Uniform Limited Partnership Act. Essentially, the two laws are quite similar. This means that there is one basic approach in the United States to the rules governing limited partnerships.

For our purposes, the limited partnership has the following attributes:

- It must file a limited partnership certificate with the state in which it is to be created. The certificate itself is fairly straightforward, and the filing fees are inexpensive. A model limited partnership form is included at the end of this chapter.

- There must be at least one general and one limited partner.

- The limited partnership need not have a limited life span. The death, retirement or insanity of a limited partner does not end the existence of a limited partnership—nor does the assignment of a limited partner's interest end the business's life span. The death, retirement or insanity of a general partner, however, can end the business's life, unless the certificate filed with the state provides that the business will be continued with new general partners.

- Although most people associate the limited partnership with real estate syndications, a limited partnership can engage in limitless types of businesses.

- General partners are held liable for the debts of the business to the same extent that they would be held liable to third persons if they were partners in an ordinary partnership. They are viewed as fiduciaries of the limited partners, which means that they must manage the business in accordance with the highest standards of good faith.

- Limited partners have virtually no role in the management of the business and are not liable to outsiders for the debts of the business.

The General Partner's Role

Although the law does not set a limit on the number of general partners a limited partnership can have, we will assume that the business will have only one general partner. The general partner's rights, duties and most importantly, liabilities, are identical to those of the partner in an ordinary partnership. The general partner makes all of the business decisions and sees to it that they are carried out. He or she bears all of the responsibility for the debts of the business if there are not sufficient assets to meet the claims of creditors.

Given the general partner's liability for the business's debts, how does a limited partnership fit into your asset protection program? This hurdle is easily overcome. First, the general partner can be a corporation formed primarily for this purpose. There is no requirement that the corporation have a specific amount of assets. In fact, most states permit a corporation to be formed with only minimal capitalization. Second, if the purpose of the limited partnership is solely to manage the assets put into it, then there is no need to fear the claims of third persons against the business. The business under those circumstances will have little if any basis on which to create debts to trade creditors or accidentally injure others.

Let us assume that you have put all of your assets into a limited partnership and that you are the general partner. You take back a one percent interest in the company and make family members the limited partners. Your personal creditors now can only go against your one percent interest in the limited partnership. But, they can only get the income which that one percent interest provides; they cannot take your place as the general partner of the business. At the same time, however, you obtain the following benefits:

- You maintain control over the manner in which those assets will be managed.

- You maintain control over the way in which the income of the limited partnership will be distributed, e.g., you can arrange to have the limited partnership pay you an appropriate salary for your services as a general partner.

- In the event of your death, the assets themselves will remain with the limited partners that you have chosen, and a properly drafted limited partnership agreement will permit the limited partners to select a new general partner. Essentially, the bulk of your assets will not have to go through probate (the one percent holding that you retained may have to go through probate).

- You've adopted a business form that restricts the federal and state taxing authorities to only one bite out of your income.

The Role of the Limited Partner

As we've noted above, the role of the limited partner is very restricted. In return for that limited participation, the limited partner enjoys complete protection against liability for the debts of the business. In fact, the only risk the limited partner runs is that he or she will lose the investment he or she may have made in the business.

As we noted earlier in our discussion of general partners, the limited partnership that is created as an asset protection tool is likely to have as its sole purpose the protection of the assets put into the business. The limited partnership, therefore, is not likely to engage in efforts that will create liability for trade debts or physical injuries to others. But, what of the claims of creditors or others against a limited partner for debts that were incurred outside of the limited partnership? Essentially, the uniform acts governing this form of business put those creditors behind a rather large eight ball.

Let's start with a look at the Uniform Limited Partnership Act and see how it words its governing provision. Section 22 of that Act provides:

(1) On due application to a court of competent jurisdiction by any judgment creditor of a limited partner, the court may charge the interest of the indebted limited partner with payment of the unsatisfied amount of the judgment debt; and may appoint a receiver, and make all other orders, directions, and inquiries which the circumstances of the case may require.

(2) The interest may be redeemed with the separate property of any general partner, but may not be redeemed with partnership property.

(3) The remedies conferred by paragraph (1) shall not be deemed exclusive of others which may exist.

(4) Nothing in this act shall be held to deprive a limited partner of his statutory exemption.

The plain English meaning of the statute is that a creditor must overcome a series of hurdles, and even then can only obtain a very limited benefit from a successful challenge.

Protecting Your Status as a Limited Partner

Since one of the major advantages of the limited partnership is its ability to immunize its passive investors from liability, it is vital that you do nothing to jeopardize that status. Limited partners can be treated as general partners if they go beyond the statutory or judicial limits of their rights. As a limited partner, you cannot take part in the management of the enterprise. Under the Uniform Acts and court decisions interpreting those acts, you are entitled to do the following:

• Act as an independent contractor for the business.

• Agree to work as an employee or agent of the limited partnership or the general partner.

- Consult with and give nonbinding advice to the general partner. However, do this sparingly and ensure that there is something in writing that demonstrates that you were supplying nonbinding advice rather than a direct order.

- Guarantee debts of the business (although this would seem to be a self-defeating gesture in an asset protection program).

- Approve or disapprove an amendment to the partnership agreement.

- Vote on the following matters:

    - the dissolution and wind-up of the business;

    - the sale, exchange, lease, mortgage, pledge or other transfer of all or substantially all of the assets of the business if the transaction does not occur in the ordinary course of business. (A real estate limited partnership that is in business to sell real property may, for example, regularly sell all of its holdings in the regular course of its business. A retail shop, however, would not sell all of its inventory and the lease on its shop in the ordinary course of its business, which is to sell goods at retail);

    - incurring debt other than in the ordinary course of the partnership's business;

    - changing the nature of the business; or

    - removing a general partner.

One other precaution: if a limited partner allows his or her name to be used in the title of the business, then that person will be treated as if he or she is a general partner.

Protecting the Limited Partnership's Tax Status

A key advantage of the limited partnership is that its profits are taxed only once—when they are received by the limited partners. The corporate form usually sees its profits taxed twice—once as profits are earned by the corporation and again in the hands of its shareholders when they receive the remainder of those after-tax profits as dividends. In one circumstance, the single taxation benefit can be lost and the limited partnership treated as a corporation for tax purposes. This happens if a corporation is used as the only general partner, and it does not have enough assets to satisfy the limited partnership's debts. If, however, your limited partnership is adopted solely to hold and manage assets, it is highly unlikely that the business will ever be in a position where it will have sufficient debts to create a problem. In such cases it is not even necessary to use a corporation as the general partner.

The use of a corporation as a general partner is usually restricted to situations where the business actively conducts activities that will create elements of risk—a real estate construction venture, for example. In such cases, the corporation that serves as a general partner must have at least $250,000 or 15 percent of the full amount of the limited partners' contributions. If the contributions total more than $2.5 million, the corporate general partner must have a net worth of no less than ten percent of the limited partner's contributions. These requirements, however, suggest that in most situations where an active business is to be run by individuals concerned with federal income tax demands, an S corporation is the entity of choice.

The Internal Revenue Service recently issued guidelines under which an entity will be recognized as a limited partnership for income tax purposes. An entity will lack the corporate characteristic of limited liability:

- If a corporation is the sole general partner, the corporation must have a net worth equal to or more than ten percent of the total equity of the partnership. If there is more than one general partner that is a corporation, the ten percent rule is determined in the aggregate—that is, the total equity of all the corporations must exceed ten percent. For purposes of calculating net worth, any ownership interest the corporation has in the partnership is not counted.

- If an individual is the sole general partner, the person's individual net worth must be worth equal to or more than ten percent of the total equity of the partnership. If there is more than one general partner that is an individual, the ten percent rule is determined in the aggregate—that is, the total equity of all individual partners must exceed ten percent. For purposes of calculating net worth, any ownership interest the individual partner has in the partnership is not counted.

- Where the general partners are both individuals and corporations, the ten percent test may be fulfilled by the corporations or the individuals, in the aggregate—that is the ten percent test may be met by any combination of net worth by the partners.

Figure 8.1   States that Have Adopted the Revised Uniform Limited Partnership Act

The following states have adopted versions of the Revised Uniform Limited Partnership Act, which the Internal Revenue Service has determined satisfies the tests for partnership treatment. States not listed may still be maintaining their statutes modeled on the older Uniform Limited Partnership Act. Check with a tax professional in your area.

Alabama:	Ala. Code sections 10-9A-1 through 10-9A-203 (Supp. 1984) effective January 1, 1984.
Arizona	Ariz. Rev. Stat. Ann. sections 29-301 through 29-366 (West Supp. 1983–84) effective July 24, 1982. Ark. Stat. Ann. sections 65-501 through 65-566 (1980) effective July 1, 1979.
California	Cal. Corp. Code sections 15611 through 15723 (West Supp. 1991), as amended through September 20, 1990, effective January 1, 1991.
Colorado	Colo. Rev. Stat. sections 7-62-101 through 7-62-1201 (Supp. 1983) effective November 1, 1981.
Connecticut	Conn. Gen. Stat. Ann. sections 34-9 through 34-38q (West 1987 and Supp. 1991), as amended, effective July 1, 1990.
Delaware	Del. Code Ann. tit. 6, chapter 17, sections 17-101 through 17-1109 (Supp. 1990), as amended through August 1, 1990.
Florida	Fla. Stat. Ann. sections 620.101 through 620.186 (West Supp. 1987) effective January 1, 1987.
Georgia	Ga. Code Ann. sections 14-9-100 through 14-9-1204 (Supp. 1988), as amended through July 1, 1991.
Idaho	Idaho Code sections 53-201 through 53-267 (Supp. 1984) effective January 1, 1982.
Illinois	111. Ann. Stat. chapter 106 1/2, Paragraphs 151-1 through 162-5 (Supp. 1989) effective July 1, 1987, with amendments effective January 1, 1988.
Iowa	Iowa Code Ann. sections 545.101 through 545.1106 (West Supp. 1984) effective July 1, 1982.
Kansas	Kan. Stat. Ann. sections 56-lalOI through 56-la601 (1983) effective January 1, 1984.
Maryland	Md. Corps. & Ass'ns Code Ann. sections 10-101 through 10-1104 (Michie Supp. 1983) effective July 1, 1982.
Massachusetts	Mass. Ann. Laws ch. 109, sections 1-62 (Law. Co-op Supp. 1983) effective July 1, 1982.

Figure 8.1 States that Have Adopted the Revised Uniform Limited Partnership Act (Continued)

Michigan	Mich. Stat. Ann. sections 20.1101 through 20.2108 (Callaghan Supp. 1984-85) effective January 1, 1983.
Minnesota	Minn. Stat. Ann. sections 322A.01 through 322A.87 (West 1982) effective January 1, 1981.
Mississippi	Miss. Code Ann. Chapter 14, sections 79-14-101 through 79-14-1107 (Supp. 1988) effective January 1988.
Missouri	Mo. Rev. Stat. chapter 359, sections 359.01 through 359.691 (Supp. 1989) effective January 1, 1987.
Montana	Mont. Code. Ann. sections 35-12-501 through 1404, effective October 1, 1981.
Nebraska	Neb. Rev. Stat. sections 67-237 through 67-297 (R.S. Supp., 1982) effective January 1, 1982.
New Jersey	N.J. Stat. Ann. sections 42:2A-1 through 42:2A-72 (West Supp. 1985) effective January 1, 1985.
Ohio	Ohio Rev. Code Ann. sections 1782.01 through 1782.62 (Page Supp. 1984) effective April 1, 1985.
Oklahoma	Okla. Stat. Ann. tit. 54, sections 301 through 364 (West Supp. 1984) effective November 1, 1984.
Tennessee	Tenn. Code Ann. sections 61-2-101 through 61-2-1208 (Supp. 1989) effective May 12, 1989.
Texas	Tex. Rev. Civ. Stat. Ann. art. 6132a-1, effective September 1, 1987.
Utah	Utah Code Ann. sections 48-2a-1 through 48-2a-1107 (1992) effective April 29, 1991.
Virginia	Va. Code Ann. sections 50-73.1 through 50-73.77. (Supp. 1987) effective January 1, 1987.
Washington	Wash. Rev. Code Ann. sections 25 10.010 through 25.10.690 (Supp. 1984) effective January 1, 1982.
West Virginia	W. Va. Code sections 47-9-1 through 47-9-63 (Michie Supp. 1984) effective January 1, 1982.
Wisconsin	Wis. Stat. Ann. sections 179.01 through 179.94 (West Supp. 1984) effective January 1, 1982.
Wyoming	Wyo. Stat. sections 17-14-201 through 17-14-1104 (Supp. 1984) effective July 1, 1979.

Role of the Corporation in an Asset Protection Program

Although the corporation plays a vital role in any asset protection program, it should not be viewed as offering complete protection in all circumstances. At most, a corporation can protect you from liability arising out of the conduct of a business. Unlike the limited partnership, the corporation will not shield your personal assets from an attack by third persons based on non-corporate debts you may have.

Corporations are entities that were created by legislatures in order to make it possible for entrepreneurs to raise money from a broad group of investors. In order to convince people to invest in enterprises that required vast amounts of capital, the legislatures introduced the concept of limited liability, i.e., the business entity—not those who operated or invested in it—would be liable for its debts. Although it is an artificial entity, a corporation is viewed as a person by the law. As an entity, it bears the responsibility for its debts. In the absence of fraud on their part, the corporation's shareholders, directors and officers are not liable for the debts of the business.

The structure of the corporation is quite simple. Its owners are its shareholders, the people who invested the money with which the corporation was created and funded. The directors are the *brain* of the corporation. Elected by shareholders, the directors establish the company's policies and appoint officers to carry out those policies.

The position taken by the legislatures that created the laws under which corporations are formed is that when people deal with a corporation, they are dealing with that entity and not its shareholders, directors or officers. This is why the corporation and not its directors, officers or shareholders is held liable for the debts of the business.

Since the corporation is liable for money it borrows and injuries it may cause, it is clearly the best form of doing business for an operating company. Whatever liability the corporation incurs simply does not pass through to its directors, officers or shareholders. But, every plus usually has its minus, and that is true of the corporation. Although we'll explain how you can surmount them, here are the negatives that you must be prepared to cope with:

Problem #1

A corporation cannot protect you from liability for injuries you may cause. A doctor who incorporates and proceeds to negligently perform an operation can be held personally liable for his negligence along with his corporation. If you operate a company car and negligently injure someone, both you and the corporation that employs you can be held liable for the injury. You are protected by the corporation when the injury is caused by a different employee. In that case, unless you contributed to the injury, only the employee and the corporation can be held liable to an injured third person.

172

Response

For the most part, if you are active in an operating business, you should take care to purchase sufficient insurance to cover potential liability for your own acts. The policy can be carried by the corporation, as long as it protects you. Even if you have adopted various approaches in this book to make yourself judgment proof, sound financial planning virtually demands that you insure against third party claims of your alleged negligent performance in your trade, business or profession.

Problem #2

Since your corporation is liable for its debts, your investment in it is at risk to those with claims against the business. Assume, for example, that you own all of the shares of a corporation that operates a dry cleaning establishment. The corporation owns all of the equipment in the store and the real estate on which it stands. Assume that those assets are worth $500,000. Assume also that your business is adequately insured, and that a claim is brought against it that exceeds the amount of the insurance. Although you personally may not be liable on the claim, the corporation's assets—valued at one-half of a million dollars—can be used to satisfy the claim.

Response

You can form two corporations: one to operate the business and a second to own the assets used by the first corporation. For example, you can form a corporation that acquires both the real estate and the equipment needed to operate a dry cleaning store and lease both the equipment and the real estate to a corporation that operates the business. If the operating corporation is sued by an injured party, its insurance will be used to cover the problem. If the insurance is inadequate, the corporation that acts as the lessor of the equipment and the real estate is not liable to an injured third party since it had nothing to do with the injury. Similarly, trade creditors of the operating corporation do not have a claim against the lessor for the debts of the lessee.

Problem #3

If you are a shareholder in your corporation (or any corporation), the shares you hold can be taken by your judgment creditors for non-business debts. Assume that you are a doctor, and you own a corporation that operates a franchised fast-food outlet. Your franchise has a fair market value of $300,000. Assume that a patient sues you for malpractice and recovers an amount in excess of your malpractice insurance coverage. Your judgment creditor now takes your franchise by foreclosing on your shares of stock.

Response

If you wish to be secure from such attacks, you have no choice but to consider placing your shares of stock in an irrevocable trust or a limited partnership. Either of these options will protect your investment, but both mean that you must sacrifice direct ownership. The limited partnership does offer you the benefit of continued income from your assets if you name yourself as the general partner of the limited partnership.

Problem #4

Many corporations are C Corporations under the Internal Revenue Code. This means that they are subject to double taxation, i.e., the profits earned by the corporation are subject to a corporate income tax, and the monies that remain after those taxes are subject to tax again when they are received as income (dividends) by shareholders. If your C Corporation is successful, the combined taxes can eat up approximately 60 percent of its profits. A partnership, by way of comparison, is not taxed; its profits flow through to its partners who are taxed at their own individual rates (28 percent maximum).

Response

Consider the approach suggested in the response to Problem #2, except that you have the leasing corporation formed as an S Corporation and the operating corporation formed as a C Corporation. If the lease arrangements between the two corporations are structured properly, it is likely that the operating corporation will have very minimal profits on which taxes can be imposed. The bulk of the profits will be earned by the S Corporation that leases the real estate and equipment to the operating corporation. Why form an S Corporation? Because for most tax purposes it is treated as if it is a partnership, but in all other respects, i.e., liability, it is treated no differently than a C Corporation. In short, an S Corporation combines the best features of the partnership and the C Corporation.

The one drawback to an S Corporation is that it cannot provide medical or life insurance benefits and deduct the premiums as business expenses (neither can a partnership). A C Corporation, however, can deduct the costs of insurance premiums as business expenses. If your operating corporation is formed as a C Corporation, it can provide those benefits and deduct the cost of providing them from its income for tax purposes.

Problem #5

Corporations cannot exist without the authorization of the state in which they are created. This means that a certificate of incorporation must be filed. If you intend to use both a C and an S Corporation, you'll have to make two filings, which can be an expensive, time-consuming process.

Response

Forming a corporation is easy, inexpensive and can be accomplished in one day. After more than a century of existence, legislatures have learned how to make the corporation accessible to business people.

Minimizing Risks Involved in Operating a Corporation

Although the corporation was expressly created by state legislatures to protect investors and operators of corporations from personal liability, there are certain precautions you must take to ensure that you do not lose that protection:

- Avoid making a personal guaranty on a corporate obligation. If you volunteer yourself as a cosigner or guarantor, you are assuming the risk that you *personally* will have to repay the obligation.

- Always sign a contract, lease, loan document or other business paper in your corporate capacity. For example, always sign as "John Smith, President, ABC Corp." Never sign just as "John Smith." If you do not indicate that you are signing for the corporation, a creditor may very well be able to show that you agreed to be liable under the agreement.

- Avoid, to the extent humanly possible, careless conduct that may create potential injury to third persons. This includes matters such as hiring qualified personnel to carry out business operations. If, for example, you hire someone to drive a delivery van, make sure that person is qualified to drive the vehicle. Don't just ask if he or she has a license; demand to see it before you hire the person. If you do not, and the person is unlicensed, you can be held liable for any injuries that he or she may cause because you negligently allowed an unqualified person to perform a duty for you.

- Always make sure that your corporation pays its taxes, be they withholding, Social Security, sales or any other form of tax. If your taxes are not paid, you as an officer or controlling shareholder, can be held personally liable to either the federal government or the state government for unpaid taxes.

- Do not authorize your corporation to pay dividends unless there are profits to support the dividend payment. If dividends are paid when the corporation is losing money, the corporation's creditors can come after the individual directors of the corporation to recover monies improperly paid out.

- If your corporation's operations have any aspect that may have environmental impact, seek out expert advice to determine whether those aspects violate state or federal law. If they do, correct them immediately. Under both federal and state law, if a cleanup is required and the corporation cannot foot the bill, directors, officers and even shareholders can be required to bear the cost of the cleanup.

Figure 8.2 Model Form for Limited Partnership

Following is a model form for a family limited partnership agreement drawn in the commonwealth of Massachusetts for the Jones family

JONES FAMILY LIMITED PARTNERSHIP

THIS AGREEMENT, of Limited Partnership is entered into on the day of   19   , by and among
, General Partner (hereinafter referred to as the "General Partner") and

(hereinafter collectively referred to as the "Limited Partners").

W I T N E S S E T H:

WHEREAS, The parties desire to establish a family structure for investing and the formation of

; and

WHEREAS, the parties herein above mentioned more fully wish to be bound together in the formation of a Limited Partnership.

In consideration of the mutual covenants hereinafter set forth, the parties do hereby agree as follows:

FORMATION AND NAME OF LIMITED PARTNERSHIP.

The parties hereto form a Limited Partnership pursuant to the provision of the Partnership Law of the Commonwealth of Massachusetts now existing and as may be hereafter amended. Except as expressly provided herein to the contrary, the rights, liabilities and obligations of the Partners and the Administration, dissolution and termination of the Partnership shall be governed by the laws of the *Commonwealth of Massachusetts.*

The Partnership interest of each Partner herein shall be considered personal property for all purposes.

NAME OF PARTNERSHIP. The name of the Partnership shall be *Jones FAMILY ASSOCIATES, L.P.* (hereinafter referred to as the "Partnership"). The business of the Partnership shall be conducted under the name of *Jones FAMILY ASSOCIATES, L.P.* or such other name or names including the name of the General Partner or any affiliate, as the General Partner may, in her sole discretion, from time to time determine. The words "L.P." or "Limited Partnership" or similar words or letters shall be included in the Partnership's name where necessary for the purposes of complying with the laws of any jurisdiction that may so require. In any event, the General Partner, when acting on behalf of the Limited Partnership, shall always designate therein that the General Partner is a corporation acting as General Partner for and on behalf of the Limited Partnership.

PRINCIPAL PLACE OF BUSINESS. The principal place of business of the Partnership shall be *100 Bellevue Street, Newton, Massachusetts,* or at such other place in the *Commonwealth of Massachusetts* as may be

Figure 8.2 Model Form for Limited Partnership (Continued)

designated by the General Partner by written notice to all the Limited Partners.

PURPOSE OF PARTNERSHIP. The purpose of the Partnership shall be to invest on behalf of the family and any other individual who becomes a member of the Partnership; and to do any and all other acts and things which may be necessary, incidental or convenient to carry out the business of the Partnership as contemplated by this Agreement and lawfully conducted by a Limited Partnership organized pursuant to the laws of the *Commonwealth of Massachusetts*. The General Partner shall be empowered to do any and all acts and things necessary, appropriate, proper, advisable, incidental to or convenient for the furtherance and accomplishment of the purposes and business described herein and for the protection and benefit of the Partnership.

DURATION OF PARTNERSHIP. The Partnership shall commence on the date that the Certificate of Limited Partnership is duly filed, and shall continue thereafter for a term of 50 years, unless sooner terminated and dissolved in accordance with the terms of this Agreement.

PARTNERS. The names, addresses and designations of each of the Partners shall be as follows:

Name   Address

   Jones

DEFINITION OF NET PROFITS AND LOSSES. The term "net profits and losses" shall mean the net profits and net losses of the Partnership as determined for federal income tax purposes by the independent certified public accountant servicing the Partnership account and selected by the General Partner, at her sole discretion.

POSSIBLE RESTRICTIONS ON TRANSFER. Notwithstanding anything to the contrary herein, (i) in the enactment [or eminent enactment] of any legislation; (ii) the publication of any temporary or final regulation by the Treasury Department; (iii) any ruling by the Internal Revenue Service; or (iv) any judicial decision that in the Opinion of Counsel would result in the taxation of the Partnership for federal income tax purposes as a corporation or as an association taxable as a corporation, then, the General Partner may impose such restrictions on the transfer of said Limited Partnership Interests as may be required in the Opinion of Counsel to prevent the taxation of the Partnership for federal income tax purposes as a corporation or as an association taxable as a corporation, including the making of any amendments to this Agreement as the General Partner in her sole discretion may determine to be necessary or appropriate in order to impose such restrictions.

Figure 8.2 Model Form for Limited Partnership (Continued)

CAPITALIZATION AND CAPITAL ACCOUNTS. The Partnership shall have an initial capitalization of   . Such capitalization shall consist of an investment by the General Partner of $, an investment by   . Said Partnership Capital Accounts are more fully set forth in Paragraph 10 herein.

An individual capital account shall be established and maintained for each Partner and shall be credited with the amount of each Partner's capital contribution to the Partnership.

The Partnership shall maintain for each Partner a separate Capital Account in accordance with the rules and regulations set forth in the Internal Revenue Code (hereinafter referred to as "Code"). Such Capital Account shall be increased by (i) the amount of all Capital Contributions made by such Partner to the Partnership pursuant to this Agreement; and (ii) all items of Partnership income and gain and decreased by the amount of cash or net agreed value of all actual and deemed distributions of cash or property made to such Partner pursuant to this Agreement and all items of Partnership deduction and loss and allocated to such Partner pursuant to this Agreement.

For purposes of computing any item of income, gain, deduction or loss to be reflected in the Partners' Capital Accounts, the determination, recognition, classification of any such item shall be the same as its determination, recognition and classification for federal income tax purposes including any method of depreciation, cost recovery or amortization used for that purpose.

No interest shall be paid by the Partnership on Capital Contribution or on balances in the Partners' Capital Accounts.

The books and records of the Partnership shall include full and true information regarding the amount of cash and cash equivalents and a designation and statement of the net value of any property contributed by each Partner to the Partnership.

For purposes of maintaining the Capital Accounts and in determining the right of the Partners among themselves, the Partnerships' item of income, gain, loss and deduction shall be allocated among the Partners in each taxable year in proportion to that percentage of ownership of the Partnership as set forth below.

INITIAL PARTNERSHIP CAPITALIZATION AND PERCENTAGE OWNERSHIP INTEREST.

Capital Contribution   Percent of Partnership Interest

Jones

Distribution of available cash with respect to any calendar year shall be made at the sole discretion of the General Partner to all Partners in the

Figure 8.2   Model Form for Limited Partnership (Continued)

proportion to their respective ownership interest as set forth in Paragraph 10 herein.

LIMITATION OF LIABILITY. In no event shall a Limited Partner become personally liable for any losses, obligations or debts of the Partnership in excess of the amount of his respective initial or any subsequent capital contribution called for by the General Partner pursuant to this Agreement, unless said debt of the Partnership is personally guaranteed by such Limited Partner. No Limited Partner shall have any priority over another Limited Partner as to the return of his capital contribution.

CONTROL AND OPERATION OF PARTNERSHIP.

Except as otherwise provided in this Agreement, all decisions respecting any matter said forth herein or otherwise affecting or arising out of the conduct of the business of the Partnership shall be made by the General Partner and the General Partner shall have the exclusive right and full authority to manage, conduct, control and operate the Partnership's business and effect the purposes and provisions of this Agreement. Except as otherwise expressly provided in this Agreement, the General Partner shall have full authority to do all things on behalf of the Partnership that it deems necessary or desirable by it in the conduct of the business of the Partnership.

The General Partner shall cause to be filed the Certificate of Limited Partnership as required by the laws of the *Commonwealth of Massachusetts* and shall cause to be filed such other certificates or documents as may be required for the formation, continuation, qualification and operation of a Limited Partnership in the *Commonwealth of Massachusetts* or any other state in which the Partnership elects to do business or own property. The General Partner shall file any necessary amendments to the Certificate of Limited Partnership including, without limitation, amendments to reflect any successor or additional General Partner and admitted pursuant to the laws of the *Commonwealth of Massachusetts* and shall otherwise use her best efforts to do all things (including the appointments of registered agents of the Partnership and maintenance of registered offices of the Partnership) requisite of the maintenance of the Partnership as a Limited Partnership under and pursuant to the laws of the *Commonwealth of Massachusetts* or any other state in which the Partnership may elect to do business or own property.

In addition to all other rights and powers, the General Partner shall have the specific rights and powers required for or appropriate for her management of the Partnership business. Such rights and powers shall include, but not be limited to, the following:

to employ persons in the operation and management of the Partnership business, including, but not limited to, employees, salesman, supervisory management agents, insurance brokers, underwriters, attorneys, and such other advisors, on such terms and for such other

Figure 8.2   Model Form for Limited Partnership (Continued)

compensation as the General Partner shall best determine, including persons or entities related to or affiliated with the General Partner;

to place title to or the right to use Partnership assets in the name of the Partnership, or in the name of the General Partner, or in the name or names of nominees for any purpose convenient or beneficial to the Partnership;

to borrow money, with or without security, and, if security is required for the repayment thereof, to execute notes, loan documents and to pledge or subject to any security device any portion of the property of the Partnership, and to pay or repay, in whole or in part, refinance, modify, consolidate or extend any loan or other security device, provided, however, that all of the foregoing shall be on such terms (including the execution of warrants of attorney to confess judgment against the Partnership with respect to obligations, if the lender demands that such a cognovit provision be included as part of such obligation) and in such amounts as the General Partner shall deem in her absolute discretion to be in the best interest of the Partnership;

to purchase, lease, develop, improve, maintain, exchange, trade or sell all or part of the Partnership assets at such price, rental or amount for cash, security or other property, and upon such terms as the General Partner in her absolute discretion shall deem to be in the best interest of the Partnership; and,

to negotiate and execute a lease and any renewals thereof for the premises upon which the Partnership's business will be located, or upon different premises, at such rental and upon such terms as the General Partner in her absolute discretion shall deem to be in the best interests of the Partnership.

The General Partner shall have no liability to the Partnership nor to any Limited Partner for any mistakes or errors in judgment, not for any act or omissions believed in good faith to be within the scope of authority conferred by this Agreement. The General Partner shall be liable only for acts and/or omission involving intentional wrongdoing. Actions or omissions taken in reliance upon the advice of legal counsel approved by the General Partner as being within the scope conferred by this Agreement shall be conclusive evidence of good faith; however, the General Partner shall not be required to procure such advice to be entitled to the benefits herein recited.

COMPENSATION AND REIMBURSEMENT OF GENERAL PARTNER.

The General Partner shall be reimbursed for all expenses, disbursements and advances incurred or made in connection with the organization of the Partnership, and the qualification of the Partnership and the General Partner to do business.

The General Partner shall be reimbursed on a monthly basis, or on such other basis as the General Partner may determine in her sole discretion for

Figure 8.2 Model Form for Limited Partnership (Continued)

(i) all direct expenses it incurs or makes on behalf of the Partnership including amounts paid to any person or persons to perform services for the Partnership as an employee of the General Partner or otherwise, and (ii) the portion of the General Partner's legal, accounting, utilities, investor, communication, telephone, secretarial, travel, entertainment, bookkeeping, reporting, data processing, office rent and other office expenses, (including overhead charges), salaries, fees and other compensation and benefit expenses of employees, officers, directors and other administrative or overhead expenses and all other direct and indirect administrative and incidental expenses in each case necessary or appropriate to the conduct of the Partnership's business. The General Partner shall determine such fees and expenses that are allocated to the Partnership in any reasonable manner in her sole discretion.

Subject to the provisions of this section, the General Partner may propose and adopt or cause to be adopted on behalf of the Partnership, without the approval of the Limited Partners, employee benefit plans.

Such expenses for overseeing the operations of the Partnership's business shall be paid without reference to the net profits and/or losses of the Partnership.

PARTNERSHIP FUNDS. The funds of the Partnership shall be deposited in such account or accounts as are designated by the General Partner. The General Partner may, in her sole discretion, deposit the funds of the Partnership in a central account maintained by or in the name of the General Partner or the Partnership. All withdrawals from or charges against such accounts shall be made by the General Partner or by its officers or agents. Funds of the Partnership may be invested as determined by the General Partner except in connection with acts otherwise prohibited by this Agreement.

LIABILITY OF GENERAL PARTNER. The General Partner may exercise any of the powers granted to it by this Agreement and perform any of the duties imposed upon it hereunder either directly or through an agent and the General Partner shall not be responsible for any act or omission on the part of herself or any such agent appointed by the General Partner in good faith if it and/or said agent act in a manner reasonably believed to be in, or not opposed to the best interest of the Partnership, and if such act or omission did not constitute gross negligence or willful misconduct on her part or the part of said agent.

OTHER MATTERS CONCERNING THE GENERAL PARTNER.
The General Partner may rely and shall be protected in acting or refraining from acting upon any resolution, certificate, statement, instrument, opinion, report, notice, request, consent, order, bond or other paper or document believed by it to be genuine and to have been signed or presented by the proper parties.

Figure 8.2 Model Form for Limited Partnership (Continued)

The General Partner may consult with legal counsel, accountants, appraisers, management consultants, investment bankers, and other consultants and advisors selected by it, and any opinion of any such person as to matters that the General Partner reasonably believes to be within such person's professional expert confidence shall be full and complete authorization and protection in respect to any action taken or suffered or omitted by the General Partner hereunder in good faith in accordance with such opinion.

The General Partner shall have the right with respect to any of her powers or obligations hereunder to act through any of her duly authorized officers and a duly appointed attorney(s)-in-fact. Each such attorney shall, to the extent provided by the General Partner in the Power of Attorney, have full power and authority to do and perform every act and duty which is permitted or required to be done by the General Partner.

TITLE TO PARTNERSHIP ASSETS. All Partnership assets, whether real or personal or mixed, and whether tangible or intangible, shall be deemed to be owned by the Partnership as an entity and no Partner, either individually or collectively, shall have any ownership interest in such Partnership Assets or any portion thereof. Title to any and all of the Partnership Assets may be held in the name of the Partnership, the General Partner, or one or more nominees, as the General Partner may determine. The General Partner hereby declares and warrants that any Partnership Assets for which legal title is held in the name of the General Partner shall be held in trust by the General Partner for the use and benefit of the Partnership in accordance with the terms and provisions of this agreement; provided, however, that the General Partner shall use her best efforts to cause beneficial and record title of such assets to be vested in the Partnership as soon as reasonably practical. All Partnership Assets shall be recorded as the property of the Partnership on its books and records, irrespective of the name in which legal title to such Partnership Assets is held.

RESOLUTION OF CONFLICTS OF INTEREST. Unless otherwise expressly provided in this Agreement, whenever a potential conflict of interest exists or arises between the General Partner or any of her affiliates, on the one hand, and the Partnership and any Partner on the other hand, any resolution or course of action in respect of such conflict of interest shall be permitted and deemed approved by all Partners, and shall not constitute a breach of this Agreement, or of any Agreement contemplated herein or therein, or of any duty stated or implied by law or equity, if the resolution or course of action is, or by operation of this Agreement, deemed to be fair and reasonable to the Partnership.

Whenever this Agreement or any other Agreement contemplated hereby provides that the General Partner is permitted or required to make

Figure 8.2   Model Form for Limited Partnership (Continued)

a decision in her discretion or under a grant of similar authority or latitude, the General Partner shall be entitled to consider only such interest and factors as it desires and shall have no duty or obligation to give any consideration to any interest of or factors affecting the Partnership or any Limited Partner or "in good faith" or under another express standard, the General Partner shall act under such express standard and shall not be subject to any other or different standards imposed by this or any other Agreement contemplated hereby.

ADDITIONAL FUNDS.

In the event that the General Partner should deem it necessary for the Partnership to look for additional funding or capitalization, the General Partner shall have the authority to borrow funds on behalf of the Partnership if in the sole discretion of the General Partner said additional funds are necessary for the performance and function of the business pursuant to the stated purpose of the Partnership herein.

If additional funds are desired, then the Limited Partners may provide said funds in the form of loans to the Limited Partnership. Said loans shall bear an interest rate as then charged by the Provident Bank of Philadelphia for commercial loans and for a period of time agreed to between the General Partner and the Limited Partners. Said funds, pursuant to the Loan Agreement, shall be repaid to the lending Limited Partner pursuant to the terms of the Loan Agreement before any distribution is made to any other Limited Partners, but in no event should said loan repayment affect any distributions to the lending Limited Partner who shall participate in distributions as any other Limited Partner.

ACCESS TO INFORMATION.

In addition to other rights provided by this Agreement and applicable law, each Limited Partner and the duly authorized representative shall have the right, upon reasonable notice which shall not be less than three business days, and at such persons own expenses, but only upon written request and for a purpose reasonably related to such person's interest as a Limited Partner, to (i) have true and full information regarding the status of the business and financial condition of the Partnership; (ii) inspect and copy promptly, after they become available, the Partnership's federal, state and local income tax returns for each year; (iii) have on demand a current list of the full name and last known business, residence or mailing address of each Partner; (iv) have true and full information regarding the net agreed value of any capital contributions made by the General Partner and the Limited Partners and the date on which each such person became a General Partner or Limited Partner; (v) have a copy of this Agreement and the Certificate of Limited Partnership and all amendments thereto, together with copies of executed Powers of Attorney pursuant to which this Agreement or any such certificate has been executed; and (vi) have any other information regarding the affairs of the Partnership as is just and reasonable.

Figure 8.2   Model Form for Limited Partnership (Continued)

BOOKS, RECORDS AND ACCOUNTING REPORTS.

The General Partner shall keep or cause to be kept complete and accurate books and records with respect to the Partnership's business which books and records shall at all times be kept at the principal office of the Partnership. The books of the Partnership shall be maintained upon the accrual basis or cash basis as designated by the General Partner and in accordance with the generally accepted accounting principals, except to the extent otherwise required herein.

The fiscal year of the Partnership shall be the calendar year.

As soon as practical, and in no event later than 120 days after the close of each Partnership year, the General Partner shall deliver to each record holder as of a recent date selected by the General Partner, reports containing financial statements of the Partnership for the fiscal year including a balance sheet and statement of operations, Partners' equity, and changes in financial position, all of which shall be prepared in accordance with generally accepted accounting principals.

The General Partner may release such information concerning the operations of the Partnership to such sources as is customary in the industry or required by law or regulation of any regulatory body.

PREPARATION OF TAX RETURNS AND TAX MATTERS. The General Partner shall arrange for the preparation and timely filing of all returns of the Partnership necessary for federal, state and local income tax purposes in the jurisdictions in which the Partnership conducts business and shall use all reasonable efforts to furnish to the record holders within 75 days of the close of the taxable year the tax information reasonably required for federal, state and local income tax reporting purposes.

Subject to the provisions hereof, the General Partner is designated as the Tax Matters Partner (as defined in Section 6231 of the Internal Revenue Code) and is authorized and required to represent the Partnership (at the Partnership's expense) in connection with all examinations of the Partnership's affairs by tax authorities including resulting administrative and judicial proceedings, and to expend Partnership funds for professional services and costs associated therewith.

RESTRICTIONS ON TRANSFER. Notwithstanding the other provisions of this Agreement, no transfer of any Limited Partnership Interest therein shall be made if such transfer (i) would violate the then applicable federal or state securities laws or rules, regulations of the commission, any state securities commission, or any other governmental authority with jurisdiction over such transfer (ii) would result in the taxation of the Partnership as a corporation or as an association taxable as a corporation for federal income tax purposes or (iii) would affect the Partnership's existence or qualification as a Limited Partnership under the appropriate Commonwealth of Massachusetts law.

Figure 8.2 Model Form for Limited Partnership (Continued)

POWER OF ATTORNEY. The foregoing Power of Attorney is hereby declared to be irrevocable. Any power coupled with an interest shall survive and shall not be affected by the subsequent death, incompetency, dissolution, disability, incapacity, bankruptcy or termination of the Limited Partnership, and shall extend to the Limited Partners' heirs, successors and assigns. Each person who becomes a Limited Partner under and pursuant to this Agreement is deemed to consent to be bound by any representations made by the General Partner acting in good faith hereby pursuant to such Power of Attorney.

Each Limited Partner is deemed to constitute and appoint the General Partner, with full power of substitution, as its true and lawful agent and attorney-in-fact, with full power and authority in its name and place instead to:

execute, swear to, acknowledge, deliver, file and record in the appropriate public offices (i) all certificates and other instruments including, at the option of the General Partner, this Agreement and the Certificate of Limited Partnership and all amendments and restatements hereof and thereof that the General Partner deems appropriate or necessary to carry out the purpose of this Agreement and to form, qualify or continue the existence or qualification of the Partnership as a Limited Partnership (or a Partnership in which the Limited Partners have a limited liability) in the _Commonwealth of Massachusetts_ and all jurisdictions in which the Partnership may or may not wish to conduct business or own property; (ii) all instruments that the General Partner deems appropriate or necessary to reflect any amendment, change or modification of this Agreement in accordance with its terms; (iii) all conveyances and other instruments or documents that the General Partner deems appropriate or necessary to reflect the dissolution and liquidation of the Partnership pursuant to the terms of this Agreement (including a Certificate of Cancellation); and (iv) all instruments (including, if required by law, this Agreement and the Certificate of Limited Partnership and amendments and restatements hereof) relating to the admission of any Partner, the initial or increased capital contribution of any Partner.

Sign, execute whereto and acknowledge all ballots, consents, approvals, waivers, certificates or other instruments necessary in the sole discretion of the General Partner, to make evidence, give, confirm or ratify any vote, consent, approval, agreement or other action that is made or given by the Partners hereunder or is consistent with the terms of this Agreement or appropriate or necessary, in the sole discretion of the General Partner, to effectuate the terms or intent of this agreement; provided, however, that when required by the provision of this Agreement which establishes a percentage of the Limited Partners, the General Partner may exercise the Power of Attorney only after the necessary vote, consent or approval by the Limited Partners.

Figure 8.2 Model Form for Limited Partnership (Continued)

STATUS OF LIMITED PARTNER.

The Limited Partners shall have no authority to conduct or control the Partnership business except as expressly provided herein, and shall have no authority to bind the Partnership in any way or manner whatsoever. No Limited Partner shall take part in or interfere in any manner with the conduct or control of the Partnership.

No Limited Partner shall have the right to demand the return of his capital contribution.

Each Limited Partnership Interest shall be fully paid for and nonassessable. No Partner shall be deemed a Limited Partner until (i) he has executed this Agreement and incorporated Power of Attorney referred to in this Paragraph 27; and (ii) he has contributed cash or other property acceptable to the Partnership, equal to the amount set opposite his name in Paragraph 10 hereof.

Irrespective of any other provision of this Agreement, no Partnership real property shall be purchased, and all or substantially all of the Partnership's property may not be sold, transferred, exchanged or traded by the General Partner without the written consent of the holders of 90% of the Limited Partnership Interests.

ASSIGNMENT, TRANSFER OR SALE OF PARTNERSHIP INTEREST.

The interest of a Limited Partner may be assigned, transferred or sold without the written consent of the General Partner and 90% of the non-transferring Limited Partners, subject to subparagraphs 29(b) and 29(c) herein. An assignor, transferor or seller of a Limited Partnership Interest may, with the consent of the General Partner, grant the assignee, transferee or purchaser the right to be a substituted Limited Partner upon compliance with the conditions set forth in subparagraph 29(c) below.

No such assignment, transfer or sale of all or a fraction of a Limited Partnership Interest shall be effective with respect to the General Partner or the Partnership, unless and until it appears, to the full satisfaction of the General Partner, that such assignment, transfer or sale will not be in violation of, or otherwise render the Partnership and/or the General Partner liable under the Securities Act of 1933, as amended, and the rules and regulations promulgated thereunder, or under the applicable state securities laws of any state or states.

Notwithstanding the preceding provisions of this Paragraph 28, no sale or exchange of all or a fraction of a Limited Partnership Interest may be made if the Limited Partnership Interest or fraction thereof sought to be sold or exchanged, when added to the total of all other Limited Partnership Interest and/or General Partnership Interest sold or exchanged within the period of twelve (12) months prior thereto, would result in the termination of the Partnership under Section 708 of the Internal Revenue code, or any successor section thereto.

Figure 8.2 Model Form for Limited Partnership (Continued)

Subsequent to the assignment, transfer or sale of a Limited Partnership Interest or fraction thereof, the Partnership shall remit directly to the assignee, transferee or purchaser all distributions to which such person may be entitled pursuant to the provisions of this Agreement.

A Limited Partner who has assigned, transferred or sold his entire interest in the Partnership, whether or not any assignee, transferee or purchaser has become a substituted Limited Partner, shall have no further right or interest in the Partnership.

No assignment, transfer or sales of the General Partnership Interest may be made by the General Partner without the prior written consent of the holders of ninety percent (90%) interest of the then outstanding Limited Partnership Interest.

RETIREMENT, BANKRUPTCY OR INCOMPETENCY OF GENERAL PARTNER.

The General Partner may elect to retire from the Partnership upon giving at least ninety (90) days, but not more than one hundred eighty (180) days notice, in writing, to the Limited Partners of her intention to do so. In the event that the Limited Partners do not elect to continue the Partnership, the Partnership shall be dissolved on the effective date of the General Partner's retirement, and the General Partner shall wind up and liquidate the Partnership as provided herein.

In the event of the bankruptcy or retirement of the General Partner, the Limited Partners may elect to continue the Partnership. In the event that the Limited Partners do not elect to continue the Partnership, the Partnership shall be dissolved in which event one or more Limited Partner shall wind up and liquidate the Partnership.

In the event the Partnership is continued, the General Partner, or the legal representative of the General Partner, shall become a Limited Partner, and shall no longer have the rights and obligations of General Partner, and the General Partnership Interest shall become a Limited Partnership Interest. Such retired or bankrupt General Partner shall be treated on the same basis as the Limited Partners with respect to the distributions and/or allocations made pursuant to this Agreement.

In the event of the bankruptcy or retirement of the General Partner, the Limited Partners may, by written consent of the holders of a majority of Limited Partnership Interest, within thirty (30) days after notice of such event, elect to continue the Partnership. The Limited Partners, by written consent of the holders of a majority of Limited Partnership Interest shall designate from among themselves or a third party or parties a new General Partner or Partners, if such designated person and/or persons shall consent to and accept such designation, the new General Partner shall succeed to all of the rights, duties and obligations of the General Partner occurring from and after the date of acceptance. In the absence of such election, consent and acceptance, the Partnership shall be dissolved on such 30th

Figure 8.2   Model Form for Limited Partnership (Continued)

day, in which event the Limited Partner or Partners shall designate from among them one or more Limited Partner or Partners to wind up and liquidate the Partnership, unless the General Partner has the responsibility to wind up and liquidate the Partnership.

DEATH, BANKRUPTCY OR INCOMPETENCY OF LIMITED PARTNER.

In the event of death, adjudication of bankruptcy, whether voluntary or involuntary, or adjudication of incompetency of a Limited Partner during the term fixed for the continuance of the Partnership, the Partnership shall not be dissolved nor shall its business terminate, but instead the executor, administrator, trustee or the legal representative of the deceased, bankrupt or incompetent Limited Partner shall succeed to the rights of such Limited Partner, subject to the provisions of this Agreement. If the interest of a deceased Limited Partner shall pass by bequest or distribution, any individual or individuals to whom the interest of a deceased Limited Partner shall have passed shall be admitted to the Partnership as a substituted Limited Partner to the extent of the Limited Partnership Interest which shall have passed to him, her or them, upon compliance with the provisions of Paragraph 33 below. A trustee or other legal representative for a bankrupt or incompetent Limited Partner may apply for admission to the Partnership as a substituted Limited Partner to the extent of the Limited Partnership Interest of such bankrupt or incompetent Limited Partner and may, by approval of the General Partner, in his sole discretion, be so admitted, upon the compliance with the provisions of Paragraph 33 below.

If a successor in interest to a bankrupt or incompetent Limited Partner is not admitted as a substituted Limited Partner pursuant to the provisions of subparagraph 30(a) above, such successor in interest shall have only such right as an assignee of such interest would have if such assignee or assignees had not been admitted as a substitute Limited Partner or Partners.

If the General Partner deems it to be in the best interest of the Partnership, it may treat, at her election, for any of the purposes of this Agreement, any successor in interest to a bankrupt or incompetent Limited Partner, who has not become a substituted Limited Partner, as a Limited Partner in the place of said bankrupt or incompetent Limited Partner.

SUBSTITUTION OF LIMITED PARTNER. As a condition to the admission of any substituted Limited Partner, such person so to be admitted shall execute and acknowledge such instruments, including the power of attorney referred to in Paragraph 27 herein, in form and substance reasonably satisfactory to the General Partner, as the General Partner may deem necessary or desirable to effect such admission and to confirm the agreement of the person being admitted as such Limited Partner to be bound by all the covenants, terms and conditions of this Agreement as the same may have, from time to time, been amended. Such persons so to be admitted as a substituted Limited Partner shall also pay all reasonable

Figure 8.2 Model Form for Limited Partnership (Continued)

expenses in connection with the substituted Limited Partner's admission as a substituted Limited Partner, including, but not limited to, the cost of the preparation and filing of any amendment to the Certificate of Limited Partnership which the General Partner may deem necessary or desirable in connection with the admission of such person as a substituted Limited Partner.

TERMINATION OF PARTNERSHIP. The Partnership shall be terminated and dissolved upon the first to occur of the following:

upon the expiration of the term of Partnership as set forth in Paragraph 5 herein;

at any time when there shall be no General Partner and a new General Partner shall not have been designated pursuant to Paragraph 29 herein;

upon the sale of all or substantially all the assets of the Partnership; or

upon written demand of Limited Partners owning a ninety percent (90%) or greater interest in the Limited Partnership Interest; provided, however, that no such demand for termination and dissolution may be made by the Limited Partners if such demand would cause a default of any loan obligation of the Partnership, or if such demand would cause a breach of any agreement to which the Partnership is a party, or if such demand would cause a breach of any Partnership obligation.

DISSOLUTION AND LIQUIDATION OF PARTNERSHIP.

Upon the expiration of the term of the Partnership or upon the dissolution of the Partnership under any of the other provisions of this Agreement, a full and general accounting shall be taken of the Partnership business and the affairs of the Partnership shall be wound up. Any profits or losses incurred since the last previous accounting shall be divided among the General Partner and the Limited Partners in accordance with the provisions of Paragraph 11 herein, and shall be added to the distribution to be made to each of the General and Limited Partners. The General Partner or Partners or Limited Partner or Partners appointed in accordance with the provisions of Subparagraph 29(c) above, as the case may be, shall wind up and liquidate the Partnership by selling the Partnership's assets and paying all the Partnership liabilities and expenses and fees incurred in connection therewith, or by distributing such assets in kind, subject to such liabilities, or by a combination thereof, as determined by the General Partner and a majority in interest of the Limited Partners. Thereafter, the balance of the proceeds, if any, shall first be used to bring the capital accounts of the Partners into balance (including marking up deficits in such capital accounts), then shall be distributed in the same manner and proportions as set forth in Paragraph 11 herein.

A reasonable time shall be allowed for the orderly liquidation of the assets of the Partnership and the discharge of liabilities to creditors so as to minimize the normal losses attendant upon a liquidation; provided,

190

Figure 8.2 Model Form for Limited Partnership (Continued)

however, that in no event shall the liquidation of the assets of the Partnership, the payment of creditors, and the distribution of Partnership assets to the General and Limited Partners occur more than one year after the occurrence of the event causing the dissolution of the Partnership pursuant to this Agreement.

Each of the General and Limited Partners shall be furnished with a statement prepared by the Partnership's accountants, which shall set forth the assets and liabilities of the Partnership as of the date of complete liquidation. The General Partner shall cause to be duly filed a Certificate of Cancellation of the Partnership.

Notwithstanding anything in this Agreement to the contrary, the General Partner shall not be personally liable for the return of the capital contributions of the Limited Partners, or any portion thereof, it being expressly understood that any such return of the capital contributions of Limited Partners shall be made solely from Partnership assets.

MEETINGS OF THE PARTNERS. Meetings of the Partners shall be held not less than five (5) days nor more than fifteen (15) days after receipt of written notice from the General Partner. The General Partner shall give notice of a meeting of the Partners at any time upon the General Partner's own choosing or within five (5) days after the General Partner shall receive written demand for a meeting from the holders of a majority interest of the Limited Partnership Interest.

AMENDMENTS. This Agreement may be amended and the observance of any terms or conditions of this Agreement may be amended only with the written approval of the holders of a majority in interest of the Limited Partnership Interest, with the consent of the General Partner; provided, however, that no such amendment may be made by the Limited Partners if such amendment would cause a default of any loan obligation of the Partnership or if such amendment would cause a breach of any agreement to which the Partnership is a party or if any such amendment would cause a breach of any Partnership obligation.

NOTICES. All notices, consents or other instruments hereunder shall be in writing and mailed by the United States mail, postage prepaid, and shall be directed to the parties hereto at the last addresses of the parties furnished by them in writing to the Partnership, and to the Partnership at its principal office. The Partnership and/or any Partner shall have the right to designate a new address for receipt of notices by notice addressed to the Partners and/or the Partnership and mailed as aforesaid. Such notices shall be made a permanent part of the Partnership records.

CERTIFICATE OF LIMITED PARTNERSHIP. The Partners, both General and Limited, shall execute, under oath, a certificate required by the Partnership Act of the *Commonwealth of Massachusetts*, if requested, and shall execute, under oath, all amendments or cancellation thereof whenever the same shall be required or appropriate.

Figure 8.2 Model Form for Limited Partnership (Continued)

BINDING EFFECT. This Agreement constitutes the entire agreement among the parties pertaining to the subject matter hereof, and supersedes all prior contemporaneous agreements and understandings of the parties in connection therewith.

GOVERNING LAW. This Agreement and the rights of all parties hereunder shall be construed in accordance with the laws of the *Commonwealth of Massachusetts.*

EXECUTION. This Agreement may be executed in several counterparts, each of which shall be considered an original when executed by the General Partner and/or one or more of the Limited Partners.

IN WITNESS WHEREOF, each party has executed this Agreement or counterpart hereof on the _____ day of _____, 19

WITNESS

_____   _____
                                           Jones
                                           General Partner

                                           _____
                                           Limited Partner

9

Questions and Answers on Asset Protection

Q. Can an IRS levy continue to take my paychecks as I earn them?

A. Yes. Section 6334 of the Internal Revenue Code authorizes a levy to be continuous until the time period has expired or the tax liability is satisfied.

Q. Can the IRS take my entire paycheck?

A. No. Section 6334(d) provides the statutory exemption to which you are entitled. The 1988 Tax Act changed the previous exemption amount and substituted the following formula:

The term *exempt amount* means an amount equal to the sum of—

- the standard deduction, and
- the aggregate amount of the deductions for personal exemptions allowed the taxpayer under section 151 in the taxable year in which such levy occurs, divided by 52.

Q. Which of my personal assets are exempt from IRS seizure?

A. Section 6334(a) lists the personal property that is exempt from IRS seizure. It includes:

- "Such items of wearing apparel and such schoolbooks as are necessary for the taxpayer or for members of his family."
- "If the taxpayer is the head of a family, so much of the fuel, provisions, furniture, and personal effects in his household, and of the arms for personal use, livestock, and poultry of the taxpayer, as does not exceed $1,650 in value."

- "So many of the books and tools necessary for the trade, business, or profession of the taxpayer as do not exceed in the aggregate $1,100 in value."

Also exempt are such property as certain pension payments to railroad workers, workmen's compensation payments and support payments to minors.

Q. How long does the IRS have to collect delinquent taxes?

A. The 1990 Tax Act extended the time the IRS has to collect an assessed tax from six to ten years. After ten years, the IRS may not proceed against your property unless you have agreed to extend the time for collection. The form granting the extension is Form 900, Tax Collection Waiver. You may find the collection agent most uncooperative if you do not consent to the extension. In fact, the agent may even seize all of the taxpayer's assets, without regard to the difficulties it places upon the taxpayer and his or her family.

Q. Can the IRS take my pension or retirement account?

A. Yes. All retirement monies, both qualified and nonqualified, are subject to attachment by the IRS. The Employee Retirement Income Security Act (ERISA) generally prohibits creditors from obtaining pension monies. The IRS is notably absent from that prohibition.

Q. How does the IRS know what I own?

A. You tell them, either voluntarily or indirectly. At collections, the collection agent will ask you to fill out Form 433 (see Chapter 4), particularly if you are asking for an offer and compromise of your liability. The IRS also has your previously filed income tax returns listing your securities holdings and interest-bearing accounts, and showing whether you take a mortgage deduction for land that you own. Older returns will also show if you had any consumer loans that may be secured by an automobile or a boat. Finally, the IRS has the authority to subpoena your records from your bank, stockbroker, accountant and anyone else they may think has records of your financial condition.

Q. Does a tax lien stop me from transferring real estate?

A. No. In general, the tax lien flows with the real estate. Therefore, the government is protected as long as the lien was *perfected*. As a practical matter, however, the buyer will probably insist that the lien be satisfied at closing.

Q. Is there any benefit in transferring real estate to my spouse?

A. With respect to a tax liability, your spouse may be an *innocent spouse*. Property in your spouse's name, as long as it is not a fraudulent transfer, will be exempt from IRS liens.

Q. Should my spouse and I file separate tax returns?

A. From an asset protection standpoint, it is advantageous to file separately. A spouse who files separate tax returns is not responsible for the tax liability of the other spouse. However, separate filings may result in a larger tax bill. This is due to the fact that the tax law rates are higher for single individuals than they are for married couples.

Q. How does the homestead exemption affect the sale of real property?

A. In states that grant a homestead exemption, the property subject to the exemption may not be sold unless the purchase price exceeds the exemption amount. Therefore, states that provide unlimited homestead exemptions are desirable places for an individual to have a residence.

Q. Can I continue to own property after filing for bankruptcy?

A. If you file for a Wage Earners Plan, you continue to own and control your assets. However, if you file a Chapter 7 bankruptcy, all nonexempt property is turned over to a trustee.

Q. What if I cannot make my Wage Earner Plan payments for a short period of time?

A. If your ability to make the required payments under the plan will continue for an extended period, the court will likely convert your plan to a Chapter 7. If the nonpayment will be temporary, however, the plan can usually be modified.

Q. When must my unsecured creditors file claims under a Chapter 13?

A. Your unsecured creditors are required to file their proof of claims within 90 days after the first scheduled meeting of creditors. If they fail to do so, your debt to them will be discharged without any payment and they will be unable to make a claim later. Remember that only your debts to creditors who are disclosed are discharged, so do not be fooled into thinking that by not listing creditors you will cause their claim to go away.

Q. Are there ways to protect family property if I must file for bankruptcy under Chapter 7?

A. Yes, your property can be effectively retained through the use of family limited partnerships, corporations and business trusts. All members of the family have some form of an ownership interest in the entity. Originally this may have been accomplished when each family member contributed assets to the business. As an alternative, the parents initially may have owned 100 percent of the entity and subsequently gifted ownership interests to their children. Ultimately the ownership interest of the parent would be reduced to zero, but he or she would still be the managing person, e.g., trustee, president or managing general partner. Since the parent has no ownership interest in the entity, there are no assets for the bankruptcy court to take. However, always be sure *not* to complete a transfer transaction within one year of bankruptcy or the trustee may void the transfers as fraudulent conveyances.

Similarly, an individual could gift away his or her property prior to the bankruptcy. The Internal Revenue Code entitles each individual to annually gift, without tax liability, $10,000 per recipient, $20,000 for married couples. Further, each individual has a lifetime credit, known as the unified credit, equivalent to $600,000 of value transferred for less than adequate consideration. Accordingly, an individual might gift up to $600,000 plus $10,000 per recipient without incurring any tax liability. Assume that a husband and wife have two married children and four grandchildren. They could gift $1,360,000 without incurring any tax liability for the gift. The amount is reached when the husband and wife each use the full $600,000 of their unified credit equivalency plus the $10,000 they gave to each child, each child's spouse and each grandchild. Subject to the earlier discussion of fraudulent conveyance, these gifts would be exempt from a bankruptcy proceeding involving the gifting parents. It is not difficult to imagine that after—or even during—a bankruptcy, the property in question would be loaned to the parents for their benefit. **Be careful! Such arrangements may be subject to scrutiny by the bankruptcy trustee.**

Q. Can my creditors seize my interest in an inheritance?

A. Usually, creditors can attach your inheritance, but not before it is distributed to you. Many wills contain spendthrift clauses so that your creditors cannot anticipate your inheritance and receive your share directly from the estate.

Q. What should I do if I anticipate a large inheritance and currently have substantial creditors?

A. You have two strategies to follow to keep your creditors from taking your expected inheritance.

1. You can disclaim the inheritance, or
2. You can file for bankruptcy before the inheritance.

When you disclaim an inheritance you are treated as if you were not alive, and your share goes to the next level of beneficiaries. If your children or your spouse are at the next level, a disclaimer will be an effective tool to shield assets from your creditors.

Bankruptcy will discharge your debts. If done more than six months before the receipt of an inheritance, the inheritance will not be part of the bankrupt estate and will be exempt from the claims of your creditors. Recently, an individual who was the sole beneficiary of a million dollar estate declared Chapter 7 bankruptcy to discharge a bank debt of $500,000. The bank was not even pressing its claim, because it was aware of the prospective inheritance. Needless to say, the bank was less than thrilled.

Q. Should I transfer my property to a trust or limited partnership instead of to my spouse?

A. There is no easy answer here. Emotional rather than asset protection concerns may prevail. The risk of divorce may negate your asset protection program. Similarly, you do not know that your spouse will continue to be the one who is less subject to creditors' claims. Finally, creditors may be successful in overturning a transfer to your spouse as a fraudulent transfer.

Q. Can I use a mortgage to protect my real estate?

A. Yes, a creditor who holds a mortgage has the greatest security in the property. All others stand in line after the mortgagee. Consider granting mortgages to family members to whom you owe money. For non-mortgage debtors to collect against your property, they will have to pay off the mortgage holders who are ahead of them.

You may consider remortgaging your real estate to strip out your equity in the property. For example, a parcel of land worth $200,000 may have a mortgage against it of $160,000. You might record additional mortgages in favor of your family for an additional $30,000. Your equity in the land is $10,000. A creditor with a $5,000 claim against you would have to sell the property and net $190,000 before he or she would realize anything from the sale.

Q. How should I protect myself from liability as a director of a corporation?

A. The primary protection available to the director of a corporation is director's and officer's liability insurance. As with most casualty insurance, this is an efficient use of dollars for the protection and peace of mind that it provides. Many corporations will offer a director an indemnification agreement. These agreements are fine as additional protection, but without liability insurance, the indemnification protection may prove valueless. If the business becomes insolvent or goes bankrupt, its directors and officers may be the owners of a worthless indemnity.

Q. Can property owned by my spouse be subject to attachment by my creditors?

A. No. Universally, the courts have recognized the separateness of ownership between husband and wife. Your property is not at risk from your spouse's creditors, and vice versa. The exception to this separate recognition is if the debt is a joint debt of both spouses.

Q. Can I be obligated to provide my creditors with a listing of my property prior to my creditors obtaining a judgment?

A. No. However, if your creditor becomes aware that you are disposing of your assets, he or she may ask the court to enjoin any fraudulent transfers. Such prohibition is an extraordinary power of the court that is exercised in only the most special circumstances.

Q. Are gifts to family members easily voidable?

A. Gifts to family members are subject to challenge as fraudulent transfers. Love and affection do not constitute consideration for a transfer. If you are insolvent after the gift, the courts will treat the transfer as fraudulent on its face.

Q. What is a spendthrift trust?

A. Classically, a spendthrift trust prohibits a creditor from reaching inside the trust to satisfy claims against either the grantors or the beneficiaries. The clause does not limit a creditor's ability to attach property after it comes out of the trust. It is only a bar to enforcement procedures while the property is in the trust.

Q. How can I protect newly acquired assets from prior judgments?

A. The primary way to protect newly acquired assets is to have them actually titled in your spouse's or children's names. If the assets are for a business venture, it would be best for all parties involved to incorporate the business with your spouse or children holding the shares of the corporation and you being employed as an officer. In this fashion, you control the day-to-day use of the assets, but they are not *legally* yours for your personal creditors to be able to attach.

Q. How should I title assets that will be used in a risky start-up venture?

A. Most attorneys recommend that operating assets be maintained outside of the corporation and leased to the new venture. Assuming that your corporation satisfies the legal requirements for formation and operation so that creditors cannot breach the corporate veil, the leased assets will be beyond the reach of creditors if the corporation fails.

There may also be tax advantages to leasing assets to a corporation. You will be receiving income from the corporation that may be *tax-free* as a result of the depreciation deduction to which you are entitled.

You may leverage additional tax benefits by placing the assets in a minor's trust. The income is payable to the trust for the benefit of your children and, if they are over 14 years of age, the lease income is taxable at your children's tax rate, which is likely to be lower than your tax rate.

Q. Should real estate be included in an operating corporation?

A. An operating corporation should never own real estate. Your operating corporation is likely to be exposed to significant claims from creditors. Real estate can be the greatest source of equity. Keep it outside the grasp of your creditors, by leasing the real estate to the corporation.

Q. Must a professional maintain malpractice insurance?

A. The answer depends on state law. Many states require professionals to have insurance. For example, it is an ethical violation for an attorney not to have insurance. The failure to purchase malpractice insurance can cause a lawyer to be suspended from the practice of law. In the past, many professionals chose to "go naked" to discourage claims. This is both foolish and foolhardy. Going naked may leave you truly out in the cold without your family home and/or other possessions. In today's litigious society, the rule should be to purchase as much insurance as possible.

Q. What is the best way to protect against risk?

A. Insurance is the most cost-efficient and reasonable way to protect the bulk of your assets from a claim. You should have the following types of insurance:

- *Automobile Insurance.* In many states the law requires you to have this insurance, but you may be surprised at how many people drive without protection because of the expense. Check with your insurance agent and purchase enough insurance to give you liability protection. You should maintain at least $100,000/$300,000 coverage, particularly if you have a home. It would be a compounded tragedy if you were in an accident, got sued, your insurance covered only $50,000 and a judgment was rendered for $200,000. The injured person would probably try to go after your home to collect his or her claim. It is this type of threat that your asset protection planning should seek to avoid.

- *Homeowner's Insurance.* Homeowner's insurance protects you from injury claims by people who are on your property. It is inexpensive, and many mortgage companies provide for it in your escrow account. One million dollars is the recommended coverage to provide for unforeseen situations.

- *Umbrella Coverage.* This is the most underutilized form of insurance; yet it is the most economical of all liability insurance. Umbrella coverage provides an additional layer of coverage on top of your current insurance. The charge is usually nominal for one million dollars of coverage. Also, ask your insurance agent if an umbrella policy will allow you to reduce your other coverage amounts—thereby saving additional money. Umbrella coverage also provides protection for items that may not be covered by your homeowner's insurance, i.e., libel and slander claims.

Index

I

Illness, catastrophic, 3
Income exemptions by state, 137–142
Income taxes, 3
Individual Retirement Accounts (IRAs), 127, 130, 131
Individual Retirement Annuities, 127, 130
Inheritance, 196
Injury
    financial, 2
    physical, 2
Innocent spouse, 98, 194
Insolvency, definition, 15
Insurance
    automobile, 199
    homeowner's, 199
    malpractice, 198–199
    umbrella coverage, 199
Installment agreement, 77–78
Installment payment arrangement, after IRS seizure, 59
Interest in property, after IRS seizure, 58
Internal Revenue Code, 57, 128, 130, 196
Internal Revenue Manual, 56
Internal Revenue Service, 1, 56–60, 128,
    collection guidelines, 85–88
    general installment agreement guidelines, 88
    levy, 193
    limited partnership guidelines, 169
    recovering property from, after seizure, 58–59
    seizure procedure, 56–58, 193–194
Irrevocable trust, 144
    establishing an, 155–161
Irrevocable minor's trust, 145–146
Isle of Mann, 147, 148

J

Joint ownership. *See* Co-ownership
Joint tenancy, 151, 152
Judgment creditor, 9
Judgment proof, 2

K

Keogh plans, 130, 131

L

Land trusts, 150–151
Law of fraudulent conveyance, 13
Levy and sale, 89–94
    general concepts, 89–90

property exempt from, 90–92
records of attorneys, physicians, and accountants, 92
safe deposit boxes, 92–94
statutory authority to, 90
Life insurance
    maximizing protection, 135
    policies, 27, 134–135
    trusts, 146
Loans
    consolidation, 26–27
    family, 26
    finance companies, 26
    home equity, 26–27, 53
    life insurance policies, 27
    pension plan, 27–29
    usurious, 54

M

Malpractice insurance, 198–199
Management by objectives, 7
Massachusetts Business Trusts (MBT), 150
Medicaid Trust, 148–149
Mortgage, 197
    negative, and the elderly, 54
    refinancing, 53
    second, 53

N

Needs, specific, 2
Negative amortization, 53
Negative mortgage and the elderly, 54
Newly acquired assets, protecting, 198
Non-family transferees, 12
Nonprotection transfers, 12

O

Offers in compromise, 59–60, 81–83, 97–100
    advising taxpayers of provisions, 97
    grounds for, 97
    investigation of, 98–99
    liability of husband and wife, 98
    public policy, 99–100
    refusal to submit financial statement, 98

P

Partnerships, and asset protection, 163, 197
    general, 164
    the general partner's role, 166
    limited, 165–166